9.50

# Essay

P9-EDR-128

# Books Reviewed

# Books Reviewed

*Critical Essays on Books and Authors*

## By J. C. Squire

Essay Index

KENNIKAT PRESS, INC./PORT WASHINGTON, N. Y.

BOOKS REVIEWED

First Published in 1920
Reissued in 1968 by Kennikat Press
Library of Congress Catalog Card No: 68- 16299
Manufactured in the United States of America

ESSAY AND GENERAL LITERATURE INDEX REPRINT SERIES

TO

IOLO ANEURIN WILLIAMS

## PREFATORY NOTE

THIS book contains a selection from papers on new and old books which have been for some time appearing weekly in the *Observer*, whose editor I sincerely thank.

J. C. S.

# CONTENTS

# CONTENTS

# JOHN CLARE

DURING the eighteenth and early nineteenth centuries there was something like a dynasty of poets whom critics specially commended to the public on the ground that they were of humble, particularly rustic, origin. There was Stephen Duck the thresher, Bloomfield the farmer's boy, Jones the Derbyshire butler. Most of these prodigies would never have been admired except as prodigies. But there was one who was positively handicapped by the manner in which critics and the public approached him. John Clare, "the Northamptonshire Peasant," a selection from whose published and unpublished works has now been competently edited and charmingly printed, was taken up and trumpeted because he could write good English and scannable lines (and had, to boot, a refined and even noble face), although he had spent his youth as a farm-labourer. Men were astonished to find that he could remind them of Thomson, Crabbe, and Burns ; but they never realised that he was a better poet than Samuel Rogers, who in that day was a sort of pope. His first book went into four editions in a year—(it was published in 1820, when he was twenty-seven), but once the curiosity had grown stale Clare was neglected. Lord Radstock, who early made himself Clare's financial godfather, continued to look after him ; local landlords, clergymen, and doctors living near Helpston intermittently remembered him ; he was often asked for poems by second-rate editors ; his first publisher

(Keats's Taylor) retained his interest. But long before his death in 1864, after he had spent twenty-seven years in asylums, he was almost forgotten, and although several editors have since his death attempted to secure him justice, he has never been properly restored to public notice. Misfortune probably drove him mad (if he really did go mad), and it has dogged him in death as in life. " The spirit of fame," he wrote, " of living a little after life like a noise on a conspicuous place, urges my blood upward into unconscious melodies." But the force of that impulse in him, the rare purity of his poetic spirit, was never recognised, and interest in him was so slight that until recently nobody cared to know that he had written an enormous mass of unpublished poetry. After this new edition (*Poems.* Selected and edited by Edmund Blunden and Alan Porter) he will not again, I think, be dismissed with a line in the histories and a page in the anthologies.

Clare was a sensitive man, and knew love, poverty, disappointment, and madness. Inevitably something of these experiences came into his verse. His great lines, beginning " I am ; yet what I am none cares or knows," commemorate his asylum years in almost every anthology. During those years he was haunted by the memory of an early love, Mary Joyce, and wrote about her often and most affectionately. How imaginative are his lines on " First Love " :

> And then my blood rushed to my face
>   And took my sight away.
> The trees and bushes round the place
>   Seemed midnight at noonday.

# JOHN CLARE

In " The Stranger " he wrote a very powerful religious poem, forgetting his own sufferings in the contemplation of Christ's. And the remembrance of things lost, one of the most constant subjects of poetry, often moved him to poetry. Childhood was gone :

> The stream it is a common stream,
>> Where we on Sundays used to ramble,
> The sky hangs o'er a broken dream,
>> The bramble's dwindled to a bramble.

At nearly forty he was moved by a benevolent landlord out of the village in which he had always lived, and " The Flitting " is a very poignant expression of his hankerings for a place every corner of which was transfigured in retrospect. The green lanes shut out the hot sun, the brook had a lovely little bridge, there were old stiles to rest on :

> And little footpaths sweet to see
> Go seeking sweeter places still.

Clare did, to some extent, write (in the ordinary sense of the word) autobiographically. But as a rule he did not greatly concern himself with human passions, nor (except when the pressure of circumstance was especially acute) with his own passions, save only his dominant passion for his native landscape.

In the nature and persistence of his love for, and his zeal to record, the commonest incidents of the life of the country, he closely resembled the late

3

Edward Thomas, though his pictures were less often tinged with the melancholy of his mind than were Thomas's. His descriptive poems continually remind one of the landscape painters of the time : sometimes of the water colourists, sometimes of Old Crome and Constable, but most often of George Morland, most rustic and most English of painters, a man who loved the thing he saw anywhere on any day, and was content to show it as it was. Lines like those on the cowboy :

Whose sun-burnt skin and cheeks chuffed out with fat
Are dyed as rusty as his napless hat,

might have been written as inscriptions for a Morland : and whatever Clare describes his exactitude is the same. There is not a season, not a month, not a common bird or beast or flower or bush or tree, not a type of building, not a type of human being in the Midlands that he knew, which is not faithfully sketched in his pages ; and the wealth of his subsidiary detail is extraordinary. There are things which we daily see, and, in an unformulated way, like daily, but which we scarcely ever find mentioned in poetry, which is rather accustomed to select its scenes and (too often) to be content with exploiting the acknowledged beauty of forms, lights, and colours, seas, hills, and sunsets, consecrated by many precedents. But with Clare we look over a common farmyard gate or walk along an ordinary field path, fully aware of all that we see : oaks, hazels, and brambles, weeds under foot, mud, grasshoppers, ants, snails

on thorns, pine-needles, the remains of a gipsy camp,
barking dogs, louts watching sheep, children picking
cowslips (" and, aye, the youngest ever lags behind"),
ducks dabbling in ponds, dogs sunning themselves,
turkeys, geese, grunting hogs, and strutting cocks.
He does not tumble his details out without discrimination. There is always cunning in his arrangement,
and he has a sound instinct for emotional signifi-
cance. Take these two brief examples from poems
on November and another on winter :

> Where dead leaves rustle sweet and give alarm
> To little birds that flirt and start away.

> Moody crows beside the road forbear
> To fly, though pelted by the passing swain.

Each of these phrases suggest far more than it says,
and they are characteristic of him. But he was largely
a poet of details, and it is for his details that one
likes him. His best whole poems are too long to
quote. But here is one of the short pieces discovered
by his present editors, " The Stonepit " :

The passing traveller with wonder sees
A deep and ancient stonepit full of trees ;
So deep and very deep the place has been,
The church might stand within and not be seen.
The passing stranger oft with wonder stops
And thinks he e'en could walk upon their tops,
And often stoops to see the busy crow,
And stands above and sees the eggs below ;
And while the wild horse gives its head a toss,
The squirrel dances up and runs across.

The boy that stands and kills the black-nosed bee
Dares down as soon as magpies' nests are found,
And wonders when he climbs the highest tree
To find it reaches scarce above the ground.

And how he loved to complete his pictures may be
illustrated with two stanzas from his long poem on
the spear thistle :

The sheep when hunger presses sore
   May nip the clover round its nest ;
But soon the thistle wounding sore
   Relieves it from each brushing guest,
That leaves a bit of wool behind,
The yellow-hammer loves to find.

The horse will set his foot and bite
   Close to the ground-lark's guarded nest
And snort to meet the prickly sight ;
   He fans the feathers of her breast—
Yet thistles prick so deep that he
Turns back and leaves her dwelling free.

Such a style, as straightforward and simple as Wordsworth's at its barest, leads inevitably to occasional
weakness of expression. You get in Clare couplets
such as :

And all expected such a rosy face
Would be her ruin—as was just the case.

But if you like Clare you do not mind that any more
than if you like Wordsworth you mind the excess-
ively plain statements of fact that you sometimes
find in him.

6

# JOHN CLARE

Mr. Blunden and Mr. Porter have begun their work well. I say " begun " because they will be compelled to do more. They state in their introduction that they selected the hundred and fifty poems here printed from two thousand which they examined, of which two thousand three-quarters (I suppose) have never been printed at all. Of the ninety new poems which they print, at least forty are as good as any of the old ones, and it is to be presumed that there are many interesting ones amongst those which, when making the present small collection, they had to reject. If anything, the general level of the new poems is higher than that of those printed in Clare's four books. The reasons for this are not recondite. Clare was at his best and most prolific in the latter half of his life after he had lost close touch with publishers and editors. And it would appear that those who published work by him preferred his least characteristic work. The editors of Annuals between 1820 and 1840 did not want his loving and most individual transcripts of the English landscape. What they wanted was poems proving that " the Northamptonshire Peasant " could cherish sentiments as refined and use abstractions as lofty as were entertained and employed by the most highly educated versifiers of the time. It is significant that almost all the best of the Poems are of the sort quoted above, poems which Clare could have written but which neither Tom Moore nor Rogers could ever have dreamed of. There are, I take it, more of these among the two thousand ; but I believe the two thousand are not all. I have heard that just as Mr. Blunden and his colleague were pluming themselves at having

7

finished their laborious survey of the ground they were surprised (I dare not say horrified) to learn that a huge new hoard of Clare manuscripts, poems, diaries, and letters, literally by the sack-full, had been discovered in Northamptonshire. There is no help for it : they must go on.

We must keep our sense of proportion. We have enough of Clare's work to be certain that we shall never think him a great poet. Even a " final " edition of him must be a selection. Clare was not a Keats or a Shelley that his feeblest fragments must be scoured for and perpetuated ; an edition of him in ten volumes would be a monument not to his genius but to an admirer's folly. But he was a far better poet than has ever been realised ; he had talents peculiar to himself ; his best work is worth looking for industriously ; and his character and career were sufficiently remarkable to justify a biography far more considerable than anything which has yet been done. A large volume of intelligently-chosen poems and a companion volume of life and letters would justify themselves, and would leave him securely established among the secondary English poets.

# MISS MANSFIELD'S STORIES

BOOKS of short stories are now rare ; books of short stories in which one can be at all interested are exceedingly rare. It is about ten years since Mr. Wells, collecting the stories of his lamented youth, commented on the fact that the short story had declined. In the nineties, when he began writing, all the most eminent, and all the most potentially eminent of English prose-writers were energetically writing short stories. Some of them may have been writing to a formula. Others, like Mr. Wells, recognised no definition, but were content to set down as " jolly " and " vivid " a record of occurrences as they could. " It may," he said, " be horrible or pathetic, or funny or beautiful, or profoundly illuminating, having only this essential, that it should take from fifteen to fifty minutes to read." But when Mr. Wells wrote the preface to his collection, the serious short story had almost disappeared, and (except for the imported O. Henry) we have had little of any interest since. The magazine writers have continued to turn out stories for their public ; the refined authors have published volumes of short pieces difficult to write and difficult to read ; but nothing has been published which has had more than an ephemeral reputation, and few things which have had even that. Stevenson and Henry James are dead ; the authors of " The Man Who Came Back " and " The Secret Sharer " seem to have exhausted their veins in this kind ; and the little masterpieces of Mr. Max Beerbohm refuse to be labelled under any category, or to be used as illustrations of any general tendency. When a respectable writer does publish a volume of what look like short stories the chances are that he calls them " studies," and that the reader who does not regard art as the best means of producing a headache will find them intolerably tedious.

Miss Mansfield's collection, *Bliss*, boldly labelled " stories," is, therefore, remarkable for not being tedious. It is far from tedious. She has so penetrating a mind and such a talent for expression that she would be interesting whatever form she were using and whatever subject she were writing about. It is not that she has a markedly personal view of things, a passionate or a philosophical attitude ; she is restrained, and leaves her affections and her admirations too much to be guessed and deduced. It is not that she has a rich prose style ; she checks the natural music in herself, and contents herself with a perpetual stream of exact statements as terse as she can make them. Every word counts to the intelligence and the eye, but none to the ear. But the fabric of her writing has no weak or dull places. She beats all the writers of dyspeptic " economical " " realistic " " studies " on their own ground. Every story is a tissue of accurate observations accurately expressed. Miss Mansfield has an extraordinary visual, and, if one may say so, olfactory, memory ; her stories may vary in reality, but her material settings—in which one includes everything from vegetation to the human garment of flesh—never. Almost every page contains minor felicities which a man with the pencilling habit would be inclined to mark.

The first few pages are crowded with them. Kezia, left behind for a few hours in the house from which her family have moved, " sat down on one of the box borders. By pressing hard at first it made a nice seat. But how dusty it was inside ! Kezia bent down to look and sneezed and rubbed her nose." Soon afterwards she is having tea with unkind and alien children :

But Kezia bit a big piece out of her bread and dripping, and then stood the piece up on her plate. With the bite out it made a dear little sort of gate. Pooh ! She didn't care ! A tear rolled down her cheek, but she wasn't crying. She couldn't have cried in front of those awful Samuel Josephs. She sat with her head bent, and as the tear dripped slowly down she caught it with a neat little whisk of her tongue and ate it before any of them had seen.

Later, she wanders over the deserted house. She finds " a pill-box, black and shiny outside and red in, holding a blob of cotton wool." " In the servant-girl's room there was a stay-button stuck in a crack of the floor, and in another crack some beads and a needle." She went downstairs and looked at the garden through a coloured glass door " at a blue lawn with blue arum lilies growing at a gate, and then at a yellow lawn with yellow lilies and a yellow fence." Beryl Fairfield, after climbing the chair in the kitchen, comes down with : " Have I got a spider's web on my face, mother ? I've been poking into that cupboard under the stairs and now something keeps tickling my nose." Raoul Duquette makes use of " a morsel of pink blotting-paper, incredibly soft, limp, and almost moist, like the tongue of a little dead kitten." Robert Salesby, imagining snow in London, saw the houses in front with " their window-boxes full of great sprays of white coral."

Miss Mansfield can bring before one's eyes any visible object, from the perspiration marks on a maid's bodice to the summer lightning fluttering " like a broken bird that tries to fly and sinks again and again struggles." And the accuracy and simplicity of her statement extends beyond this to whatever non-material state she may wish to describe. She continually delights with images such as that in which she sets down the silence between bachelor friend and spinster friend over teacup and fire in " Psychology " : " That silence could be contained in the circle of warm, delightful fire and lamplight. How many times hadn't they flung something into it just for the fun of watching the ripples break on the easy shores ? " and that in which she shows a woman's dreams reawaking when she meets the exasperating, but much travelled, man to whom she had been engaged six years before : " As he spoke, so lightly, tapping the end of his cigarette against the ashtray, she felt the strange beast that had slumbered so long within her bosom stir, stretch itself, yawn, prick up its ears, and suddenly bound to its feet, and fix its longing, hungry stare upon those far-away places. But all she said was, smiling gently, ' How I envy you ! ' " How satisfying the descriptions of mind and of matter are blended might be illustrated from any of these stories. One may take a few sentences from the picture of Beryl

Fairfield, an Anglo-Saxon—happily very Anglo-Saxon—Madame, or Mademoiselle, Bovary:

> In the dining-room, by the flicker of a wood fire, Beryl sat on a hassock playing the guitar. She had bathed and changed all her clothes. Now she wore a white muslin dress with black spots on it, and in her hair she had pinned a black silk rose. . . . .
>
> She played and sang half to herself, for she was watching herself playing and singing. The firelight gleamed on her shoes, on the ruddy belly of the guitar, and on her white fingers. . . .
>
> "If I were outside the window and looked in and saw myself I really would be rather struck," thought she. Still more softly she played the accompaniment—not singing now but listening. . . . "The first time that I ever saw you, little girl—oh, you had no idea that you were not alone—you were sitting with your little feet upon a hassock, playing the guitar. God, I can never forget. . . ." Beryl flung up her head and began to sing again:
>
> "Even the moon is aweary . . ."
>
> But there came a loud bang at the door. The servant girl's crimson face popped through.
>
> "Please, Miss Beryl, I've got to come and lay."
>
> "Certainly, Alice," said Beryl, in a voice of ice. She put the guitar in a corner. Alice lunged in with a heavy black iron tray.
>
> "Well, I have had a job with that oving," said she, "I can't get nothing to brown."

This scene lingers in the memory. And there are

others which will do that ; gardens, rooms full or empty, firelit and glittering with candles and silver, an oily singer at his piano, a decayed actress getting out of bed, groups of wondering helpless children, a Paris street, a train rattling a little frightened governess through the night. The trouble is that, generally speaking, one remembers little more than pictures, large or small. One has looked at a series of these. They have dawned on the darkness, grown bright, and quietly faded. But very seldom has one been moved. Very seldom has one felt the faintest impulse to laugh, cheer, or cry. Why ? The people are not quite real enough and not quite enough happens to them.

It isn't that Miss Mansfield is naturally a mere quiet note-taker, or that she belongs temperamentally to that depressing class of people who think they have done the finest thing in the world when they have described several articles of furniture and exhibited a phantom " he " or " she " incapably yearning, frustrate, or disillusioned. " Sun and Moon " is a delicious, a pathetic, and beautiful story, which might have resulted from a collaboration of Tchekov and Hans Andersen. In " The Man Without a Temperament " her detail is at its best, and she uses the most inconspicuous " events " to produce a beautiful and exalting impression. Generally, however, interested as one is, one doesn't much care what happens, and very little does happen. In the first long story, very remarkable as a series of photographs, the people are, except at moments, seen clear but out of contact with us, through a glass. We leave them where they started. Either this was meant to be the beginning of a novel, or else the author was under the influence of the theory that it is cheap and vulgar to let anything happen in a narrative. Sometimes she seems to remember the other theory that if anything does happen it ought to be unpleasant. The conclusions of " Bliss" and " The Little Governess " are illustrations of that. It is not that the episodes are in themselves unlikely or uncommon. Girls often are assaulted, and husbands often are unfaithful ; but these stories (the indications given of these characters) do not prepare one for the endings. Had Miss Mansfield changed the last page of each, and prevented the catastrophes, we should never have suspected that Harry was a disloyal husband, or the old German an old satyr. It is a pity that " Bliss " thus fails to come completely off. The scenes are drawn with consummate precision, the wife is less shadowy than usual, and there are moments lyric in their intense beauty. Everything powders when we have the feeling that a realist is playing tricks with reality.

But, with all its limitations, this is a book one is bound to respect, if, possibly, one is not certain to re-read it. The author's powers have greatly matured since she wrote her first book. Her outlook, too, has modified : she is no longer at her best, and most enthusiastic, when writing of what she hates. We may hope that in the future she may be inclined to write more about the things she loves. Let there be calamity, but let us at least be moved by it ; it is depressing to read of miseries and never turn a hair at them because the author has refused to abandon herself in sympathy. Let Miss Mansfield's materials remain what they are. One does not ask her to write of pirates or cowboys, murders, burglaries, or financial ramps. Childhood and the domestic interior are her favourite haunts, and her imagination will always take her back to them. But she can afford to let herself go more, to abandon a theoretic restraint which is foreign to her, to reflect on the truth that the literature which obtains and keeps a hold on people does not make its principal appeal to the recognising eye or even to the understanding. Nobody ever said—or if he did the company must have gaped—that he found " The Trojan Women " or " Pickwick " " interesting." And what happens to people who rely too exclusively on the treatment, however masterly, of incidental detail may be illustrated from this volume. Three times in the course of the book " a piece of iron banged " meets the eye, and from two several stories I make these two extracts :

> . . . he began to do his exercises. Deep breathing, bending and squatting like a frog and shooting out his legs.
> . . . he began to do his exercises—deep breathing, bending forward and back, squatting like a frog and shooting out his legs.

The better it is done the more one remembers it and the less effect it has the second time.

# A BOOK-COLLECTOR

THERE was a brief period when Dukes in person used to contest at Sotheby's for early-printed books, whilst their friends stood around backing the respective staying-powers of their fancies as men a little while ago backed those of Carpentier and Dempsey. In our time those Dukes who have the desire presumably haven't the money. Book-collectors of a kind are as numerous in England as ever, but few rich men are among them, and nine-tenths of the really expensive books that are sold go to America. There is a class of business-man there of whom we have only a few specimens here. They are rich, they are successful in Wall Street or the stock-yards, and they are prepared to pay any price for Corots or Caxtons. Their motives are often discussed by English people. Journalists frequently describe them as men who, since titular honours do not exist in America and dreams of an O.B.E. cannot, therefore, be entertained, find the possession of a unique collection of books or pictures the best way of gaining a spurious distinction. It is not an adequate explanation. In 1509 an author wrote of the book-collector :

Still am I busy bookes assemblynge,
For to have plentie it is a pleasant thynge,
In my conceyt, and to have them ay in hande,
But what they mene I do not understande.

America then had only just been lit upon, and if we

ascribe (as some do) the American rage for book-collecting to a mere desire to have things that other people value, there is an element of that in all collecting, and men who buy what they do not understand are found everywhere. There are collectors who read in America as there are elsewhere, and some have been scholars. Perhaps a more nearly average specimen of the class is Mr. Edward Newton, who has now written a book, *The Amenities of Book Collecting*, and let in a little light upon the motives and enjoyments of some of those Americans who have, in a generation, put the price of a good First Folio up to £10,000 and given a new value to every scrap of paper written by any man of letters, dead or alive, who was ever taken seriously.

Mr. Newton is not, by modern American standards, a collector of the first rank. He is, or regards himself as, a man of modest means, who indulges his hobby as far as he is able. He has no First Folio and no Gutenburg Bible. But if he were rich enough he would, he says, buy those books at any price, and he complacently tells us (an American opinion on the point is worth noting) that for books of this kind " the sky is the limit." All books have risen enormously during his lifetime, and they will all go on rising. But, in spite of his restricted means, he has managed to collect many remarkable things under the noses of the Huntingtons and Wideners. He rambles with pleasant garrulity from author to author, and date to date, making no attempt to give a systematic account of his library ; but the " items " he mentions by the way are sufficiently numerous to give an indication of what it is like. Here are some of them—openly bought from the best booksellers : a first edition of Herrick, Wordsworth's copy of " Endymion," twenty-one presentation copies of Dickens, early works by Swinburne and Hardy, the MS. of " Far From the Madding Crowd," a holograph prayer and letters by Dr. Johnson, an unpublished work by Mrs. Thrale, presentation copies of Stevenson, Thackeray, Joseph Conrad, Johnson, and Byron (inscribed by Queen Victoria), Keats's folio Spenser, Rossetti's drawing of Tennyson reading " Maud " to the Brownings, Beardsley's drawing of Wilde, first editions of Blake, Browning's copy of Coryat, an inscribed copy of Walton's " Lives," Congreve's copy of the first " Robinson Crusoe," a first edition of " The Vicar of Wakefield," MS. poems by Lamb and Southey, fine copies of Surtees and Alken, a copy of " The Life of the Prince Consort," given by Queen Victoria to Sir A. Gordon, and a copy of " Pagan Poems," given by Mr. George Moore to Oscar Wilde.

The list is indicative both of Mr. Newton's tastes and of his dislikes. He is promiscuous enough within certain limits. But he has few really old English books, and he is thoroughly indifferent to early-printed books, which he refers to casually as " Aldines and Elzevirs," ignoring the fact that physically they are, as a body, the most beautiful books in the world. It is true that he says he buys books that he can read : and that most early books are (not that one would read them if they weren't) in Greek and Latin. But I doubt if he habitually peruses " The Life of the Prince Consort." The truth comes out in his confession : " I collect as I can human-interest books." If he could find an Aldine Cicero which (say) Fanny Brawne had given to Claire Clairmont he would pay any money for it. He reads a great deal, and his tastes are marked. He cannot care very much for verse or there would be more early poets in his library ; his own candid sentence runs : " I have always liked Pope. In reading him one has the sense of progress from idea to idea, not a mere floundering about in Arcady amid star-stuff." His favourite book is Boswell, his heroes are Johnson and Lamb : there are none better. But he does not restrict his collecting to the literature he likes, and he cannot plausibly pretend that Sir Theodore Martin is among his favourite authors or Beardsley an artist to whom admirers of Lamb are naturally drawn. The fact is that he has a passion for possessing little fragments of people's lives, an interest in relics, anecdotes, glimpses of character. Most is known and most survives (generally speaking) of men near our own date, and contemporary fashion partly dictates to Mr. Newton what he shall collect. If Mr. Beerbohm's " Enoch Soames " were suddenly decided to be both real and important, Mr. Newton would be the first in the field for an autograph copy or an agreement between Soames and his publisher. He would then be able to look cheerfully at his shelves and feel that a fragment of this illustrious dead man's universally familiar life reposed on his shelves. It is, *au fond*, the same passion as that which led the reverent Mayor to frame and glaze the butt-end of the cigar which King Edward had thrown on the station platform, and the piece of toast in which the Royal teeth had made a semi-circular identation.

Personally, I do not share that taste. I like first editions of books in which I am interested, and I covet Keats's Spenser. But I no more want (what Mr. Newton possesses) Charles Lamb's letters to Miss Kelly, the actress, than I want a lock of Shakespeare's hair (scarce as it seems to have been even in his lifetime), or one of Napoleon's bedroom slippers. Manuscript poems, yes, or prose by certain people ; but not the MSS. of any and every author whom other people think good. Still, I can understand the taste ; and, whatever a man collects, the zest of the chase is the main thing : the excitement of putting up the quarry and the satisfaction of returning home with one more pelt. There is nothing either meritorious or discreditable about a pursuit like Mr. Newton's. There is a sort of book-collector who perform services, and valuable services, to literature and history. It is largely through their means that books have been preserved which would otherwise have been lost, that our museums have been fed with a stream of rare and valuable works, that editors have been able to develop the useful science of bibliography and to standardise texts. Had it not been for this body of sentimentalists, hobby-riders and hoarders, the early editions of many of our great writers, by these secluded and cared for, would have utterly disappeared. The collections of plays made by several American collectors, the complete collection of Stevensons made (at prodigious cost) by young Mr. Widener, who went down with the " Titanic," are done with

a public as well as a private object : and I have
never understood why people should resent collections being made by Americans, who share our speech
and our past, and cannot be expected to content
themselves with the works of Washington Irving
and the pictorial inscriptions of the Aztecs. But
much of the collecting of Mr. Newton and men like
him serves no object except to please him (surely a
harmless one), and to disappoint persons in this
country (who are few) who share his mania for scraps
of autograph and find that they cannot stand up
against his purse.

But I should add one word. There was a third,
probably not a preconceived, object with Mr.
Newton : that of writing a book about his collection
and its acquisition. The result justifies him. His
book, though one sometimes gets a little tired of the
perpetual dollars, is full of amusing gossip and odd
stories, and the chapters on authors in whom he is
especially interested (above all that on Boswell) are
full of sense and pleasantly haphazard information.
Many of his illustrations add charm to the pot-
pourri. Anybody with a touch of the collector in
him or the slightest fondness for the gossipy kind
of literary history will find him readable. But neither
he nor anybody else has yet written the classic of
book-collecting or autograph collecting. The formidable works of the Rev. T. F. Dibdin, so popular
once in the palmy days of English bibliophily, are
now unreadable, partly because of the shifting of
taste and partly because of the intolerably rhapsodical
verbosity of Mr. Dibdin's style. Burton's " Book-
Hunter " is very good, but very scrappy. We still

wait the thorough history of a fine collection, which several men in England and America (Mr. Wise is an example) could give. To write that classic a man must have inexhaustible curiosity and a good memory, erudition and humour : it will contain very little literary criticism, but much human nature and many extraordinary tales. For there is no end to the strange adventures that books have had or the strange places in which they have been found, and in the history of mere bibliography, matter of types, spacing and pagination, there are detective stories more elaborate and ingenious than those of Poe.

# EDITING SHAKESPEARE

THERE was a clear case for a new critical edition of Shakespeare. Had knowledge remained where it was in the eighteenth century there would have been constant new editions, but small need for them. It was an amusing occupation to take Shakespeare's obscurer words and sentences one by one and suggest other words as those which he probably wrote, and the pastime occasionally gave an emendation splendid in its ingenuity, such as the famous " 'A babbled of green fields " for " A table of green fields." It was also amusing to compare all the early texts, and, where they differed, to choose the punctuation or the phrasing which the critic would have used had he been Shakespeare. But there could be little real progress until critics were agreed as to the respective authority of the various texts, and even agreement on that (were no more discovered) could not in itself carry as much farther. In our own day, however, the development of the bibliographical and calligraphical sciences has placed us in the possession of apparatus without which even the ablest of the old editors were at a great disadvantage. Mr. Pollard has demonstrated that in all probability the " good Quartos " were printed from Shakespeare's MSS. at his instructions, that he supervised his publications during his lifetime, and that the editors of the First Folio were acting specifically as his literary executors. Mr. Pollard and Mr. Simpson have made it plain that the punctuation, which to the mere reader often appears absurd in its vagaries, was deliberately contrived as a guide to the proper speaking of the words. The scientific comparison of the various sorts of plain errors which occur in the texts has given a clue to the nature of Shakespeare's handwriting, and thus to the solution of other errors which have puzzled everybody. Over and above this Sir E. Maunde Thompson has attempted to show (and the Cambridge editors appear to think, as I diffidently do myself, that he has proved his case), that the British Museum possesses a manuscript play, part of which is in Shakespeare's handwriting. Finally, critics in our days have, or can make, use of men who have a technical knowledge of printing and binding which their predecessors lacked, and which may unravel many small mysteries.

The results of all this may, of course, be exaggerated. Nothing very revolutionary can happen to the great mass of Shakespeare's lines, because (fortunately) they are quite well as they are. We do not find in the new Cambridge edition a mass of revolutionary notes, for there is no need for them. The editors, in fact, have wisely kept both the speculative, textual, and the purely explanatory notes down to the minimum necessary to elucidate the play. But the nature of some of their notes, which I may illustrate with a few specimens, would make Dr. Johnson rub his eyes :

155, *decked*. Generally explained as " sprinkled," but N. E. D. gives no support. Read *eked*, *i.e.*, increased (v. N. E. D. and *M. V.* 3. 2. 23) ; Prospero's tears added salt to salt. Shakespeare probably wrote " eekt " with an oversized initial, and the compositor took it for " dekt." v. T. I., p. xli. and cf. *e* and *d* of " rule " and " bid," Facs. l. 5.

100, *Who having into truth*, etc. Much annotated, and clearly corrupt. Read *minted* for " into," and the whole context gains. . . . The misprint may be explained thus : Shakespeare wrote " minted" with one or two minims short, and with the *ed* like *oe* ; this the compositor read as " inntoe," or " intoe," and set up as " into " !

367, *be quick thou'st best*. Absence of punctuation denotes rapid delivery.

91, *O, defend me !* A space on the F. [Folio], before " O," suggests that the word " God " has been omitted because of the blasphemy laws.

The new methods, of course, still afford a good deal of room for the play of editorial fancy and for disputes between experts. But they are likely to settle many problems hitherto not certainly soluble, and the succeeding volumes of this edition should contain many agreeable surprises.

One cannot here go into the details of the editors' treatment of the text of " The Tempest." There is less scope for their beneficent efforts here, as there has been less for the misguided zeal of the old emendators and text-constructors, for the simple reason that the Folio supplies our only text of the play. But there is no element of the fantastic in the notes, and the accompanying essays are admirable. Mr. Wilson writes a textual introduction, there are short treatises on punctuation, on " The Tempest," on the copy used for " The Tempest," and on its stage history. There is a glossary, and, since it is the first volume, there is " Q's " general introduction to the series. This essay is ideal for the purpose ; it is both interesting and amusing in itself and a perfect assurance that the editors are equipped with the best weapons and will use them with that taste and common sense without which the best weapons are liable to be dangerous. Sir Arthur, in repeating the old story that Shakespeare " never troubled himself or anybody to collect, correct, and print " his plays, is ignoring the conclusions reached in Mr. Pollard's recent "Shakespeare's Fight with the Pirates " ; otherwise every word he says commands assent.

Finally, I just remember to add, the volume contains a play by Shakespeare ; not the greatest, but perhaps the most nearly perfect of them all. Flawlessness is not a quality that can be generally found in him by anyone who is not a blind worshipper ; and it is a pity that the recognition of the faults without which he would have been superhuman has generally been left to his enemies, the people who have no relish for life or do not like poetry. As Sir Arthur Quiller-Couch says, he " had often to do odd jobs, was often careless, and sometimes wrote extremely ill." But in this play there is nothing that jars, little that puzzles. It was probably written more easily than anything he did, but he scamped nothing of it. He tackled the problem of telling, in the space of a few hours, a story which covered many years, and the right way came to him in a flash at last. " Another part of the same island," " another part of the same island " : the delicious scenes, all matched in scale and charm, succeed one another like a string of equal pearls ; and the whole play leaves nothing behind but a delicious fragrance on the air. The characters are not " worked out." Prospero, Alonso, Sebastian—they are just sufficient for this kind of play. Ferdinand and Miranda are the faintly-tinted, delightful lovers of a pastoral, the prince and princess of a fairy-tale. Stephano, rich as he is, has not the solidity of the earlier broad comic figures. Caliban is the only one whose mind provokes one to speculation, and even he (poor monster) will not bear the load that Browning imposed on him. They are all in tone with each other and with the wedding Masque that was surely (if the main play was earlier) interpolated for the nuptials of Elizabeth of Bohemia. There is no real conflict, little serious meditation about things ; it is a golden tissue for which all description is inadequate, and which, nevertheless, is so soundly conceived and woven that any sort of performance of it—even so (I don't speak offensively) homely and haphazard a production as that at the Aldwych—must please the person who is capable of being pleased by it at all. It may have been Shakespeare's swan-song, and would certainly be a dramatically effective one.

But can we be sure that it was consciously so ? Men frequently state, as though it were a known fact, that " The Tempest " (paradoxically so-called) is Shakespeare's placid farewell. He had gone through a period of storm and stress. He had doubted with Hamlet and Macbeth, raved with Lear and Othello ; he had questioned divine justice and human fidelity, contemplated the abysses of existence and of evil ; and, after years of distress verging on mania, had won peace and paid his final respects to the world in a fantastic play in which wickedness was scarcely serious, the triumph of good never in doubt, and all ended happily. " Here," they conceive him as remarking, " is the outcome of it all. At one time I asked many questions and received few answers. I was tortured and I groaned ; I was bewildered and I cried against the scheme of things. My passions weakened ; I became reconciled ; I was content to take the things I had ; I sailed into a calm after the storm ; I laid my blessing upon all things ; and I broke my wand." Particularly as to the breaking of the wand they have found in Prospero the symbol of Shakespeare's self : everything he wished for was accomplished, and the need for further effort was gone.

This may all be true : we cannot say that it is not. But it is as well to remember that hypothesis is not the same thing as fact. " The Tempest " was, beyond doubt, one of Shakespeare's last plays (for sentimental purposes we can pretend that we know it to be actually the last), and beyond doubt he did retire to Stratford on a competence. But if he deliberately broke his wand he was the first and last poet in the world who ever did so at his age. He must have been preternaturally prescient if he knew that he would die at the age of fifty-two, owing (as is supposed) to the insanitary conditions of the neighbourhood : and he must have had a mental constitution unique in the world's history if, after writing a succession of masterpieces, he decided point blank that he would never write another line. Poets are not usually made like that ; when they are moved they cannot usually help themselves. And poets do not necessarily go through a rounded arc of experience which leaves them in middle age beyond possibility of further change. We may, it is hardly necessary to say, run risks in assuming too close a connection between Shakespeare's experience and his themes. Men are not necessarily leading miserable lives when they are writing tragedies, nor complacent lives when they are writing comedies. But even if we do assume that connection, that " serene that Men call age " is one thing, and the exhaustion of emotion and ambition at fifty is another. Shakespeare, as a matter of fact (so far as we can discover from internal and external evidence), was always a man outwardly equable and companionable ; " the gentle unjealous Shakespeare," Mr. Bridges has called him, and the conception is traditional. That is not the sort of man who changes much, and, by all analogy, such a prolific writer is not the sort of writer who ever stops writing. He was probably at any time of his life temperamentally capable of both tragedy and comedy ; he probably was so at the end. Need we assume that he ever actually did lay down his pen ? It is surely conceivable that in retirement at Stratford he at least toyed with new plays and may have begun, or even completed, new poems. After the funeral, Anne Hathaway—who had never been taught that publication was very profitable and had not heard of the autograph market—destroyed them as what she called "a lot of old rubbish." Should some of them come to light and prove to be as sombre as " Hamlet," a great deal of conjectural biography would be destroyed.

# WILLIAM JAMES'S LETTERS

THE author of "The Principles of Psychology," son of one of the most robust and eccentric theologians and brother of Henry James the novelist, led a more active and diversified life than commonly falls to the lot of philosophers. He began as an art student, then contemplated becoming a printer, went up the Amazon on a zoological expedition, took to medicine, was successively professor of physiology, of psychology, and of philosophy, travelled widely, met half the most eminent men of his time, and died leaving a name familiar to tens of thousands. The career testifies to that essential personal element in him which he referred to when he said that what Henry of Navarre's soldiers followed was his white plume. But beyond his adventurousness, zest for life and versatility, he had a quality equally infrequent in the schools : a relish for and a gift for crude fun. This may have been a last exasperating straw to those who could not bear his doctrines ; conceive Aristotle or Kant signing a letter to his mother, " Your bold, your beautiful, your Blossom." But it has merits in the subject of a biography, and this collection of letters joined by a commentary is as readable a book as has been published for years.

There is very little polemic or exposition of philosophy in the letters printed in these selections which Mr. Henry James, jun., has made. They are personal, not professional, letters. James's main interests are, naturally, often reflected in sentences or paragraphs. A well-known passage in " Varieties of Religious Experience " concerning emergence from profound pessimism is given here as a record of the crisis in James's own life (aet. 27), and there is an interesting note of that date : " My first act of free will shall be to believe in free will." We find in 1879 a curt reference to the beginnings of the work on which his fame was to be chiefly built : " I am writing (very slowly) what may become a text-book of psychology " ; and two pages after there is a characteristic remark about one battalion of his life-long foes :

My ignorant prejudice against all Hegelians, except Hegel himself, grows wusser and wusser. Their sacerdotal airs ! and their sterility ! Contemplating their navels and the syllable *oum !*

In 1882 he tells his mother that there are few genuine philosophers about, " and I really believe that in my way I have a wider view of the field than anyone I've seen (I count out, of course, my ignorance of ancient authors)." In 1885 he writes : " There is no such superstition as the idolatry of the Whole " —a sentence often echoed by him, notably in his description of the monist's universe as a " blockuniverse " and of the monist himself as " wallowing in a sense of unbridled unity." In 1904 he tells Professor Holhous to

take the sterilest scientific prig and cad you know, compare him with the richest religious intellect you know, and you would not . . . give the former the exclusive right of way.

In the same letter is a striking example of the phraseology which maddened some people :

> Your distinction between " spurious " and genuine courage reminds me a bit too much of " true " and " false " freedom, and other sanctimonious " come-offs."

" I have," he writes in that year, " no living sense of commerce with a God. I envy those who have." Casual conversational remarks of this sort are frequent ; they will be of great interest to those who read them in the light of his books. But if the letters have any " influence " it will not be through these, but through the example they show of a life lived honestly and with gusto. Their main interest derives from the reflection of that life, from the vivid and warming picture of an interesting family circle and a variegated circle of friends, and from the perpetual shower of anecdote, serious and comic description of daily events, brief judgments on men and affairs, which proceeded from James's lively fountain of a mind. One can but illustrate these by a few random specimens.

To current politics there are few references. He wrote in 1870 that " if Alsace-Lorraine be taken, there must be another war," and in 1871 that " the German Liberals will have the harder battle to fight at home for the next twenty years." He hoped, later on, that the Boers and the Filipinos would win their wars, and he was indignant about the condemnation of Dreyfus. But the political things which really interested him were of a less momentary kind. Everybody knows how largely his brother Henry was preoccupied with differences in national character and in the qualities of various civilisations. It was a natural preoccupation in an American familiar with Europe, and William shared it. His examinations were less subtle than Henry's, and his views (especially about the Germans) fluctuated a good deal. At one moment he is bowed in admiration before the Germans ; at another, exasperated by their solemn verbosity, he is referring to " the human, as distinguished from the German mind." He never was drawn to the French, and he seems to have come with some reluctance to the conviction that the English (whom he found the only non-American people capable of blushing) were the people most to his taste. Against all of them he contrasted America, raw America, confused, uneducated, self-satisfied America, America full of " bald-headed young Ph.D.s, boring each other at seminaries." He felt the tug which pulled Henry to Europe and kept him there, but he was resolved to stand by his own country and help in shaping a future which he was certain would be great.

A preoccupation with the future, with the continued adventure of mankind and the enlargement of the bounds of knowledge, is reflected in his comments on books. James was a voracious reader, but he does not seem to have been very fond of pure literature, although his taste was fairly good. There are few criticisms of novels or poems, and these are short. He was greatly impressed by Turgeneff, was interested by " Daniel Deronda," and found Sir Walter Scott " a dear old boy." He preferred authors who bestowed the graces of literature on works of religious or philosophic interest. His criticisms on these are full of interest. He found in Emerson " too little understanding of the morbid side of life " ; of Goethe he said, " There is a deal of *naïveté* in the old cuss." Mr. Arthur Balfour's " Foundations of Belief " he thought worth fifty German books : " It almost makes me a Liberal-Unionist " ; and he described Mr. Chesterton as " a tremendously strong writer and true thinker, despite his mannerism of paradox." An ampler portrait is that of Renan :

> So the magician Renan is no more ! . . . The queer thing was that he so slowly worked his way to his natural mental attitude of irony and persiflage, on a basis of moral and religious material. He levitated at last to his true level of superficiality, emancipating himself from layer after layer of the inhibitions into which he was born, and finally using the old moral and religious vocabulary to produce merely musical and poetical effects. That moral and religious ideals, seriously taken, involve certain refusals and renunciations of freedom, Renan seemed at last entirely to forget. On the whole, his sweetness and mere literary coquetry leave a displeasing impression, and the only way to handle him is not to take him heavily or seriously. The worst is, he was a prig in his ideals.

The most elaborate piece of purely literary criticism in the letters is addressed to his brother Henry. Mr. Philip Guedalla has recently divided Henry's career into the three periods of James I., James II, and the

Old Pretender. It may be presumed, from William James's vehement abuse of his brother's "third manner," that this dynastic arrangement would have pleased him. But Henry was unperturbed. One of the early references to Henry (1867) contains the phrase "the serene Harry dealing his snubs around." To the onslaught of forty years after the serene Harry replied that if he found that his books were pleasing William he should begin to grow seriously alarmed about their merits. The relations between these two throughout the book are delightful ; the years of separation never in the least impaired their affectionate intimacy ; each immensely admired the other and thought him (we may suspect) slightly comic.

I leave it to more competent people to discuss what has happened and will happen to James's ideas. During his lifetime there were those who revered him as a Copernicus of philosophy and those who detested him as a picturesque and perverse disseminator of false notions, a " journalist " even—to use the term which (alas), in modern intellectual controversies, is always supposed to convey the last opprobrium. That his " popular " vogue, for what it was worth, would pass was inevitable ; for the large dabbling public he is no longer the latest " stunt." In 1910, the last year of his life, James met for the first time the man who, as (shall we say ?) a subject of the higher kind of dinner-table conversation holds now the place which James held fifteen years ago. " I hope," he wrote, " that Freud and his pupils will push their ideas to their utmost limits, so that we may learn what they are. They can't fail to throw light on human nature ; but I confess that he made on me personally the impression of a man obsessed with fixed ideas." The impression was correct ; and James can have found little of " the white plume of Henry of Navarre " about that most cumbrous and humourless of plodding mono-maniacs. He could " make nothing " of Freud's dream theories. Yet if he were writing now he would certainly have to take cognisance of Freud, he would certainly have to admit a core of truth within Freud's cocoon of dreary fantasy, and he would, I imagine, be forced to admit that Freud's discoveries must lead to some modification in his own picture of things : for instance (I walk diffidently on such ground) by introducing a new restriction of the area which he regarded as open to free choice by the consciousness.

The one thing certain is that whatever happened to his theories (in the way, not of what he thought crass opposition, but of genuine supersession) he would not mind. He would cheer the advance of creative evolution. For he was not the ambitious constructor of a pet, a sacred, system, but a frank, fearless, and jolly man who loved Life and was at its service. In the whole of these two volumes of letters there is not a selfish, a cruel, a priggish, or a dull sentence. His philosophy, in spite of the wide and salutary influence of the spirit behind it (described by his enemies as American Commercialism, American Uplift, etc.) upon the lay public, has never obtained much of a hold upon the academic world. Those systems which do seldom obtain much of a hold (are in fact regarded as awe-inspiring gibberish) everywhere else ; and, anyhow, all our systems, however elaborately logical, will die, as James's will, and their instructive mummies will be ranged in that mortuary catacomb which we call the history of thought. But James, at lowest, was certainly a landmark in the progress of psychology ; even his least defensible propositions had the great quality of stimulating thought ; and whatever might happen to his theories, both his works and these letters will continue to be read for the simple reason that they are delightful reading, and that their author was one of the most fascinating and lovable characters in the American record. There is always a place for the philosophic writer, however pragmatical, who does not give one a headache. And there is a great deal surely to be said for one who, seeing all the furniture in his room leaping at the shock of the San Francisco earthquake, felt " no fear, only admiration for the way a wooden house could prove its elasticity," and glee over the vividness of the manner in which such an " abstract idea" as " earthquake " could verify itself into sensible reality.

# BAUDELAIRE

MR. SYMONS'S essay on Baudelaire is slight and rather disappointing. It has faults not usual in his books. Even those who do not approve his attitude towards art and life or, usually, share his critical admirations, must admit that he has generally been a lucid critic, careful of his English and careful of his form ; exercising, in fact, that fastidiousness and aiming at that perfection which delight him in his favourite artists, whether poets, dancers, or music-hall performers. His "Baudelaire" is scrappy ; it lacks shape ; it is neither a " life " nor a thorough study. It is (if I may use the offensive words inoffensively) padded out with a chapter on Villiers de l'Isle Adam which appears to have been written long before the rest of the book and has no obvious connection with what goes before and after; and its English is remarkably rough, grammatically and otherwise, if judged by the standard Mr. Symons himself has set. The bibliography is useful. There are a certain number of " facts " in the book which will be interesting to those who are unfamiliar with Baudelairean literature ; and the reader who likes the flavour of a bygone fashion may derive some entertainment from the delightful obstinacy with which Mr. Symons maintains his desperately detached attitude towards the seven sins and the seven thousand diseases. He, whatever may happen to the rest of the world, is not going to be thrown off his balance by considerations of morals and hygiene. He sings the old tune which has strayed on from

the days of Gautier's "Moi je fais émaux et
camées." How charming a perversion ! How beautifully *stated* a brutality ! How harmonious a blasphemy ! But, granted his point of view, Mr. Symons
has often been very penetrating and illuminating,
and he might, with a greater expenditure of trouble,
have written at least the most interesting thing about
Baudelaire in English. And a good book about
Baudelaire would be welcome.

For Baudelaire was one of the most fascinating
personalities of his century, and, historically, one
of the most influential. I use the word, of course, in
a restricted sense. The large public never heard of
him, and his " teaching " was never sufficiently
coherent, or " practical," or " social," to inspire
group activity. He never disseminated drug taking
as others have disseminated vegetarianism ; no
body of his disciples has ever instituted the systematic worship of Satan or consumption of hashish in
any Hampstead Hothouse Suburb ; and the devotees
of despair remain unorganised. But he was important
both as symptom and as agent. In him there came
to a climax that romantic pessimism which had
wept in Werther and raved in Manfred, and brought
gall to the lips of some of his French predecessors ;
and there was something in him which was in none
of the others. He was the father of the later deca-
dence, and much greater than any of his children.
Classifications apart, his literary influence has in-
disputably been immense. His disciples have come
to him one by one in the solitude of their own
chambers, but those who bear his marks are found
in all civilised countries, and have included many

of the most conspicuous men of their age. Verlaine, Mallarmé, Rimbaud, Samain, Huysmans, in France : Swinburne, Wilde, Beardsley, in England : these are only a few remembered casually of the swarm whose thought and language have borne those unmistakable stigmata. It is possible to be affected by his thought, and then to cast off the sinister enchantment ; it is possible to read him without being infected by his pessimism at all. But it is impossible to read him and forget him, to hear his accents without sometimes echoing them, to turn away with indifferent eyes from his powerful and mysterious personality. It is not the actual events of his life that exert this sway. His career was no pageant. He was an affectionate son, he had a long and wretched attachment to a stupid woman of colour, he translated Poe, wrote for the newspapers, despised women, hated Belgians and material progress, was a slave to hashish, and died terribly : there is little more to be said. His power resided within himself and in the poems which came nearest to being an expression of himself. As man and artist he was wholly unlike anybody else.

It is commonly said that Romanticism is distinguished by the desire for " escape " : that " Over the hills and far away " is the phrase which best expresses the romantics of all ages and the whole romantic movement of the last century. That passion was present in Baudelaire in its intensest form ; but peculiarly. He did not, as did some of our Pre-Raphaelites, turn his back on the contemporary world. He looked hard and long at it ; he saw it vile and filthy, and described the foulness he saw with dreadful realism. He was not one of those who avoid life and find happiness by lapping themselves in dreams of things more beautiful and serene, countries of content beyond the horizon and ages golden through the haze of time. He hankered rather than escaped. He was perpetually longing for something " remote from the sphere of our sorrow," but he could never surrender himself to a vision of it ; for his eyes were open, and he saw a horrible world and a black universe, terribly anarchic or terribly governed. When he was a young man he made a voyage to the East, and the memories of it haunted him all his life. The hot blue skies, the basking islands, the brown girls, the ships lying under the palm trees, the odours of spice and of brine : they recur in his work continually as symbols of all things unattainable. But we may be sure that when he was in the East he got little consolation from them, and he was sure of it himself. In one of his prose poems (I quote Mr. Symons's own old and excellent translation) he traversed the whole world in imagination, and it all turned to dust and ashes. " Life," he said, " is a hospital, in which every patient is possessed by the desire of changing his bed. . . . It seems to me that I should always be happy if I were somewhere else." But he offers his soul Holland, and Lisbon, and the Baltic, and the Indies, and his soul remains unresponsive. In the end : " At last my soul bursts into speech, and wisely she cries to me, ' Anywhere, anywhere, out of the world.' "

His spirit had, he knew, the power of poisoning all that it contemplated. He was, he said in one of his poems, the peer of Midas ; he could turn gold into dross and built sarcophagi in the gleaming fields of heaven. He was endowed at birth with a passion for " the place where you shall never be ; the lover whom you shall never know " ; his life was spent in the pursuit of a Beauty defined by himself as inaccessible. Yet there the passion was. He might, in life, vainly attempt to distract himself with every vice. He might talk blasphemy about God and cynicism about human love. He might expend all the resources of his unique art on the description of the repellent objects which fascinated him. He might peer into every forbidden room, and defile every altar. He might walk, in the flesh or in imagination, through the most sterile of deserts and the most fetid of marshes, through all the disordered nightmares of the drug, and all the squalid byways of the human city, taverns, and brothels, and rain-soaked cemeteries ; he might profess indifference to pain and admiration for evil ; but he could never kill his unsatisfied heart, and, above the confusion, he could always perceive the glimmer of virtue and love and peace beyond his reach :

Des Cieux Spirituels l'inaccessible azur,
Pour l'homme terrassé qui rêve encore et souffre,
S'ouvre et s'enfonce avec l'attirance du gouffre.

Neither physical debauchery nor philosophic diabolism could long distract him from the unattainable ideal, and it is this which is one of the chief sources of his undiminished power of commanding men's attention and even affection. It is easy enough to detect pose or feebleness in the ordinary decadent ; and Baudelaire's own works have made thousands of such. We are tempted to say to them, " Stop this nonsense," or " Take some healthy exercise," and conceive their cases as sufficiently dealt with. Baudelaire cannot be dismissed like that. It is not possible to despise him, and we are not able to suppose that he failed to understand anything : he did not pose, there was no medicine for him, and he was as familiar with the thoughts of others as with his own. Fifty years after his death he still speaks in the portrait printed in the common edition of his poems. We see those dark liquid penetrating eyes looking out from under the contemplative forehead, the wide shut mouth, the pouting under lip. There is pride in it that tells us we are to expect, in conversation, no confessional flow, no appeal for pity ; nothing but courteous, precise, ironic sentences, acute brief analyses, observations slightly tinged with a bitter humour. But the soul in reserve is evident in the fixed, ardent, melancholy look. He suffered and he was strong. When he died of general paralysis, locked up in a body without speech, his condition was an image of his whole life. He was always a prisoner beyond reach of human contact, and the lips in his portrait seem to say that wherever he may find himself he will be the same on earth or in interstellar space, in heaven or in hell, a wanderer, a solitary and an alien. There was power in him, the power of a great personality ; but his strength was strangely manifested. There is a story by himself with a hero whose impotence was " so vast " that it was " epic."

His one resource—it can be explained no more

and no less in him than in any other—was his art, and his genius as an artist was so extraordinary that his influence would still have been great had his character and " subject-matter " lacked their peculiar qualities. He wrote impeccable prose ; but his verse, for compactness, for accuracy, for music, cannot be surpassed. He may not be ranked with the world's greatest poets : humanity will scarcely concede that to a man whose principal work was labelled (not without reason) " Flowers of Evil," and who was successfully prosecuted for obscenity : apart from which, volume of work and universality of appeal are bound to count in such matters. But there certainly never was a poet who said with more perfection what he had to say, who had fewer weak lines or otiose words, who was more consistently near his own highest level of achievement. His sense of form was like that of the great masters in marble and bronze, and he worked like a slave in his narrow field, watering it with his sweat " pour extorquer quelques épis." Here, at any rate, his influence cannot but have been salutary. If the Symbolists trace to him the origins of their " correspondences" and their mystical minglings of the senses, the Parnassians were certainly as much in his debt for the example he set of artistic self-discipline. To read him is to contract a disgust with looseness and diffuseness. It is perhaps significant that the memorial ode which the young Swinburne wrote on him was the most clear, vivid, and truly classic of all Swinburne's poems.

# KEATS

JOHN KEATS died in 1821. He was born on October 31, 1795, his father then working in a livery-stable in Finsbury Pavement. His parents died before he left school. He entered at Guy's, became a dresser there when he was twenty, met Hunt, Haydon, and Shelley in the same year, and published his first volume when he was twenty-one. " Endymion " appeared when he was twenty-two, " Lamia " and the " Odes " when he was twenty-four. He died at Rome of consumption at twenty-five, and his death was noticed in " Blackwood " as that of " a young man who had left a decent calling for the melancholy trade of Cockney-poetry."

Throughout the last hundred years Keats's reputation has steadily grown. There were those among his friends who realised when he was alive that he was a poet of extraordinary powers. That is in the natural course of things ; for in spite of the common delusion to the contrary, and the obvious truth that great writers often take many years to impress the ruck of critics and attract the general literary public, the records show that, at a very early stage in their careers, they may usually rely on recognition from a few, and especially from their colleagues. Leigh Hunt notoriously admired Keats ; Shelley, if he did not fully understand him, died with " Lamia " at his breast ; Lamb met him and told Crabb Robinson that he put " St. Agnes' Eve " next to Wordsworth. There is surely something significant in the fact that he should, at so early an age, have drifted, however casually, into the society of these men and others as eminent. They differed about his early performances, but they felt instantly in him a candidate for immortality. Outside recognition was certainly slow. Tennyson and his circle at Cambridge proclaimed his greatness as far as their voices could carry, which was not very far. He had been dead nineteen years when the first " collected " reprint appeared, and this went into remainders. Yet it did appear, and with the success of Lord Houghton's edition of 1848 came the evident fulfilment of his quiet prophecy : " I think I shall be among the English poets after my death."

The view was not, however, as yet general that he might possibly, had he lived, have been the greatest English poet after Shakespeare. Tennyson repeatedly said this, but it was not common doctrine, Attention for many years was largely centred on the things which he did supremely well ; the things completed and perfected, " Isabella," " St. Agnes' Eve," the " Odes," a few sonnets and songs, the finest passages from the longer works. His character as a poet was, as it were, fixed by these ; he excelled in visualisation, in a languorous music, in richness of imagery; for ideas, for philosophy, for doctrine, for contemplation of the nature and destiny of man in general, as for the study of men in particular, we must go elsewhere. These were not for Keats, who preferred Greek legends and autumn leaves, musical sighs, a sweet melancholy, and the shining of moonlight through a window dyed azure and gules. This view arose, as we have said, through too exclusive a study of his acknowledged masterpieces ; more recently, the examination of his outlying works and of his letters has produced a general tendency to speculate on what he might have done rather than to describe what he actually did. Not everybody has been convinced by the South African professor who has discovered a profound and comprehensive philosophical system hiding like a mighty stone temple within the tangled greenery of " Endymion " ; but there is no need to go chasing after allegories to become apprised of the fact that Keats had the attributes of an original and masculine thinker. His curiosity and his strong common sense are shown everywhere in his correspondence, and the later " Hyperion " is the work of a " world-poet " trying his mighty wings. He might, it is now conceded, have written on the Miltonic scale with the Miltonic force, though it does not seem likely that he would have driven home the Miltonic conclusions. He had a natural interest both in metaphysics and in ethics, though he was not in the habit of employing those words ; and the combination of qualities, mental and physical, in him was so rich and peculiar that had he produced " serious " works on the major themes they would have been very unlike anyone else's. As it was, he had just developed (to use his own phrase) the " large utterance of the early gods," when he died, having scarcely had the use of it. This truth is now accepted, it may even be that it has been overstated : and it is not only the seeds of a great philosophic poet, a sunnier Lucretius, that they have found in him. Critics of our own day have also argued that only time was needed to make him one of the noblest of poetic dramatists. The contention is based solely, but not altogether unreasonably, on the impressive fragment, " King Stephen," which moves convincingly and contains characters who are strongly and surely drawn and differentiated. All Keats's " potentialities " are now studied ; no writer who ever died in youth has ever had his promise explored with more wonder or more praise.

Nevertheless, though the probable greatness of Keats's maturity is now realised, we are still habitually blind to the peculiar greatness of his immaturity. We are accustomed to think of Keats, Shelley, and even Byron as poets of the Romantic age who died equally young. There is something to be said as to their relative chances of development had they all lived longer ; but leaving that aside, we commonly forget that Keats had several years of life fewer than Shelley, only half Shelley's length of manhood. Keats died at twenty-five ; at twenty-five he had created all that body of work which we have, and established the most widespread and fruitful poetic influence of the century. His poems, less numerous than Shelley's though they are, are compared with his, and people who admire both are content to differ about their respective merits. Suppose, though, that Shelley had died at twenty-five ? There would have been no " Cenci," no "Adonais, " no " Prometheus," no " Cloud," no " Skylark," no " Ode to the West Wind " ; few of the best lyrics and, of the longer poems, nothing notable except " Alastor " and " The Revolt of Islam." Byron, dying at twenty-five, would never have begun " Don Juan " ; Milton, had he died at Keats's age, would be known to us only by " Comus," " L'Allegro," " Il Penseroso," " The Ode on Christ's Nativity," and a few minor poems. Of all the great English poets only Coleridge had written the larger part of his best work before his twenty-sixth birthday, and Shakespeare himself, so far as our very inadequate knowledge extends, had written literally nothing at all, and almost certainly not a line of the plays and poems which we know. It may be suggested that the more sensuous and pictorial kind of poet may be expected to produce art of a high order at an earlier age than other men. Whether this be so or not, Keats was, in fact, not one of several equal prodigies, but a prodigy unparalleled for volume of masterly early achievement.

We may, therefore, say that even now it is not universally recognised how unique was his promise and, in the circumstances, his performance. But that he was potentially one of the greatest of all poets is a commonplace, and our own time has also seen the dissipation of a false conception of his character which imputed to him weaknesses of a kind which are not, and cannot be, found in the greatest poets, though they may be found in many poets of the second order. The greatest poets, however repugnant we may find some of them, have not been cowardly or unmanly : but for generations men thought of Keats as a querulous and hyper-sensitive, indolent and luxurious, invalid. Byron's uninformed jest about his having been " killed off by one critique " was for long current, and Shelley's marvellous but misleading elegy supplied apparent confirmation. It is now clear that Keats was as

undisturbed by the scurrilous philistinism of
" Blackwood " and the " Quarterly " as we should
expect a poet of his powers to be, except in so far
as he feared that reviewers might prevent him from
earning money—a mundane consideration, no doubt,
but even poets want their breakfasts, and cannot
always obtain them on credit. When this slander
had been finally blown away, the letters to Fanny
Brawne were published, and hundreds of critics,
including the austere and self-contained Mr. Swinburne, diffused the contempt they felt for a young
man who could so thoroughly abandon himself to
his passions. " Fulsome and liquorish endearments":
thus spake the author of " Anactoria " concerning
some of Keats's less happy lines, and of the letters
he said :

> While admitting that neither his love letters,
> nor the last piteous outcries of his wailing and
> shrieking agony, would ever have been made
> public by merciful or respectful editors, we must
> also admit that, if they ought never to have been
> published, it is no less certain that they ought
> never to have been written ; that a manful kind
> of man or even a manly sort of boy, in his love-
> making or in his suffering, will not howl and snivel
> after such a lamentable fashion.

" He lived long enough," was Swinburne's conclusion, " only to give promise of being a man."
But this misconception has been dissipated like
its predecessor. It is quite true that the sentences
which the reviewers quoted from Mr. Buxton

Forman's edition to the horror of the public and Mr. Swinburne are there : but their " piteousness " and grossness have both been absurdly exaggerated. They are as they stand, not half as " deplorable " or abnormal as they were made out to be, and the worst of them came from a man already enveloped in a mortal illness. If there are those who can guarantee what their deportment would be during that slow and painful approach to Death which may be in front of any of us, I can only say I envy them ; and the torment was very great for Keats, who was dying young, with his ambitions unfulfilled and his love unsatisfied. If we knew nothing of him beyond his verse, strength of character could be deduced from the robust power and serenity of parts of his verse ; but all the evidence we have confirms the impression. He was, when in health, sociable, humorous, sensible, intellectually adventurous : and he gave known proofs of that physical courage which may be the unmistakable manifestation of that moral courage with which it is often falsely contrasted.

To this truth after a century his countrymen have at last come. He had, most obviously, irritating faults of expression. There are vulgarisms in his early works which send shudders down the spines of the sensitive. They are almost all of one kind : they occur when he is writing of women and love. Now they would not be there, it may be admitted, had not Keats had, like most men and almost all poets, a powerful strain of sensuality. But what is objected to is not really his morals (which are often in strongly sensual men unexceptionable), but his manners : not a particular grossness in him, but his naïve and uncultivated way of confessing his proclivities. It is all a matter of words : we do not like the " dalliance " and the " fondling," the " breasts of cream " and " gentle squeezes," and, above all (to quote the most uncomfortable line from all " Endymion "), " those lips, O slippery blisses." To some extent in the early, though not in the later Keats, we feel a slightly over-marked preoccupation ; but it wouldn't have been noticed had he learnt reticence. And it is easy to guess why it took him so long to shed his vulgarisms—for that is what they were. The Leigh Hunt circle, valuable as its enthusiasm was to him, was not impeccable in its taste ; and before he entered that circle Keats in all likelihood kept precisely the company in which refinement in certain regards would be least cultivated. We can imagine him during the " apothecary " days with facetious Dick Swivellers as the most enlightened of his acquaintance, and spending much of his time with precocious young bucks like Mr. Smallweed, who ordered his chop so maturely in Chancery Lane, while casting an expert glance at the barmaid. Before Keats died his vocabulary had become civilised, and his intellect had made an advantageous pact with his senses. An article on him to-day can be ended, probably without surprising anyone, with an extract from the present Poet Laureate which indicates the measure of the change, in Keats's regard, which has come over English criticism. " If," says Mr. Bridges :

I have read him rightly, he would be pleased, could he see it, at the universal recognition of

his genius and the utter rout of its traducers ;
but much more moved, stirred he would be to
the depth of his great nature, to know that he was
understood, and that for the nobility of his character his name was loved and esteemed.

But what Gifford and Jeffrey would think is beyond
all conjecture.

# AUSTIN DOBSON'S ESSAYS

MR. AUSTIN DOBSON* has throughout his career led a double life. One of his lives has been spent in our own age, and even, to a large extent, in the Board of Trade. The other has been spent, very innocently, in the eighteenth century, and it is scarcely an exaggeration to say that he has as many acquaintances in the eighteenth century as in the twentieth, and that he is as much at home with those as with these. It is easy enough to become familiar with the outstanding figures of the Georgian era. We may know our Burke and our Gibbon, our Goldsmith, our Gray, our Reynolds, and our Sheridan. We may, through Horace Walpole and Boswell, establish some sort of contact with Conway, Mason, Mme. du Deffand, and the Misses Berry, with Bennet Langton, Topham Beauclerk, Mrs. Thrale, and General Paoli. But Mr. Dobson has penetrated far beyond those obvious circles which are the first to receive the casual traveller. He does not greatly bother about the foreground except in so far as it gives clues to the background. He has an affection for those who were persons of some, but not very much, importance in their own day ; he knows his way about a variety of cultivated middle-class homes of that bygone age : houses where the great were but casual visitors, libraries in which intelligent rentiers wrote treatises on syntax, boudoirs in which young ladies composed precocious novels or wrote sprightly letters to their

* Mr. Dobson's lamented death has happened since this was written.

friends, drawing-rooms in which harpsichord and flute were played nightly and a call from the Muscovite Ambassador caused an immense flutter. He is sufficiently familiar with the masterpieces of the age ; it would not be easy to stump him on " Amelia " or " Humphry Clinker," or " Clarissa Harlowe." But others do justice to these, and Mr. Dobson prefers to spend his time among the neglected, though never among the stupid. He will do justice to the intelligent doctor whom Dr. Johnson once met at Streatham, or the Female Sage whom Walpole casually mentioned to Sir Thomas Mann. He will dig out their works, discover their letters, pry (if he can) into their diaries, reconstruct their houses and gardens, recover their loves, friendships, ambitions, and disappointments, and. in the end, give us a picture of them in convincing relation to their contemporary setting. He cannot bear to think that a charming, a clever, or a very eccentric person should be entirely forgotten ; that is, one who belonged to the generation towards which he himself is temperamentally drawn because of its tastes, its manners, its common-sense, and its wit. In his series of books on the eighteenth century he has drawn a large gallery of such portraits, and he is now so familiar with his ground that the mention of even the obscurest of Georgian worthies at once brings into his mind half-a-dozen forgotten persons with whom " the deceased " was probably or certainly in communication. And he knows something instructive or amusing about each one of them.

His latest volume (*Later Essays*, 1917-1920), which appears after his eighty-first birthday, contains

six long essays and a few scraps of prose reflection and metrical epigram. One of the essays
deals with the Abbé Edgeworth, the Irish priest
who accompanied Louis XVI on the flight to
Varennes and knelt on the scaffold over his head-
less trunk. The subjects of four of the others are
William Heberden, " Hermes " Harris, " the learned
Mrs. Carter," and Thomas Edwards. It would be
difficult to say which of these is now the most widely
remembered, if such a term can be applied to any of
them. I suppose Elizabeth Carter, who was one of
the most sensible talkers of her time, was a blue-
stocking without being a prig, wrote several tolerable poems and a few lines that deserve preservation,
and made a translation of Epictetus, which had a
vogue (for such were the proclivities of the time) like
that of " Reynard the Fox " or " Kim " in our own
time. But the best-known person does not necessarily make the best subject. Harris serves Mr.
Dobson as well : a Wiltshire gentleman, an amateur
philologist, and father of that Lord Malmesbury
who brought Queen Caroline over to the Prince
Regent, to be received as if she were something
boring to the point of being nauseous. Dr. Heberden's career as physician and man of the world is
very typical : a sort of parallel to Arbuthnot's,
except that Heberden had no literary genius. But
Thomas Edwards, obscurer still, is responsible for
an essay full of the most delightful things. He was
a barrister of means, a friend of Richardson and
Hawkins Browne the parodist ; and his little fleet-
ing fame came with his pamphlet attacking the over-
bearing bully Bishop Warburton, the rashest, if not

the stupidest, of all Shakespeare's editors. Many of Edwards's cunning hits are recorded here, with a mass of minute information about his private life : amongst other things we are given excerpts from his ironical " Canons of Criticism," such as :

I. A Professed Critic has a right to declare, that his Author *wrote* whatever He thinks he *ought* to have written ; with as much positiveness, as if He had been at his elbow.

VII. He may find out obsolete words, or coin new ones ; and put them in the place of such, as He does not like, or does not understand.

IX. He may interpret his Author so ; as to make him mean directly contrary to what He says.

The case for the conjectural emendation has never been more succinctly put.

This resuscitation of ancient gossip is always agreeable ; but it is as well to have a present reminder that even in the eighteenth century men differed, and that the conventional picture of solid brick houses, Chippendale and chamber music is misleading. Under the crust was Gin Lane, and Walpole's excursions around his bric-à-brac were sometimes rudely interrupted by menacing multitudes of unemployed " weavers." The most memorable of these papers is of a kind less frequently represented in Mr. Dobson's collections : it deals with the career of a great and an effective reformer. John Howard, " the philanthropist " (since Dickens and Mrs. Jellyby nobody applies that noble name to a man in a wholly serious and complimentary way), was not the sort of person who wrote polemical tracts about Shakespeare, who translated elevating maxims from the ancients, who craned his neck to appraise the ceilings of Angelica Kauffmann, or who assuaged his melancholy with the strains of the German flute. He had, it is true, in early life a taste for pictures ; but once he had become convinced of the need for prison reform he never again thought of anything but prisons. The story Mr. Dobson tells is the story of one of the most austere, saintly, "dedicated," and systematically vagrant of lives. Howard was an upholsterer's son, who inherited a competence. At twenty-seven he married his elderly landlady ; she died two years later, and, grown restless, he wandered through Portugal and France. Returning, he became a member of the Royal Society, settled in Buckinghamshire and married again. He travelled a good deal (amongst other things taking the temperature of Vesuvius), and became sufficiently prominent in his rural district as to be made High Sheriff of his county. This was in 1773 ; he was forty-seven ; and up to that date he had done so little that, had he died then, nobody now living, excepting Mr. Dobson, would have heard of him. But his duty brought him into contact with the local gaol, and the gaol of that time was the foulest of foul dens :

> In it, young and old, hale and sick, pure and impure, innocent and guilty, were herded and huddled, without distinction or occupation ; and here, for the most trivial offences, on the vaguest evidence, they were detained indefinitely, in order

to satisfy the exorbitant claims for fees made by rapacious wardens and turnkeys. They were exposed to the most wanton cruelty, systematically starved, savagely punished, and ruthlessly exposed to the horrors of infection. Not a few of them became imbecile or insane, while others succumbed to the terrible distemper generated by the total neglect of sanitary precautions.

From that time to his death Howard spent most of his time scouring the prisons and pest-houses of Europe and endeavouring, through Parliament and the Press in this country and interviews with the great abroad, to secure their reformation. He spared his body no labours ; his abstemiousness was such that he would have been thoroughly at home at the table of John the Baptist. The things he saw were revolting. " His very notebook grew foul and tainted." " At Nottingham he found that the poorer prisoners slept in damp ' dug-outs ' forty-seven steps down, cut in the sandy rock. . . . At Ely it had been the practice to chain the inmates to the floor on their backs, with a spiked iron collar about their necks, and a heavy bar over their legs. . . . At Plymouth there were two small chambers for felons. One of these—the ' Clink '—was solely lighted and ventilated by a wicket in the door, seven inches by five, and to this contracted breathing-hole the prisoners under sentence of transportation came by turns for air." It sounds a ghastly condemnation of contemporary civilisation ; but it was true of those evils, as of many, that few people were enterprising enough to discover that they existed. Howard shocked the public, and received the thanks of the House of Commons. It was, as usual,. some time before anything effective was done, and after the first horror had passed there was a tendency on the part of the authorities to take the will to reform for the deed. But the reform of prison hygiene and discipline in this country (by no means perfect yet) dates from Howard, and his activities spread everywhere, from Ireland to the Urals. He repeatedly toured Spain, France, the Netherlands, Germany, Switzerland, and Bohmeia ; protested against the iniquitous " Piombi " at Venice and the treatment of prisoners of war in Dunkirk, saw the knout used in Moscow, and caught jail-fever in Lille. Forty-seven thousand miles he covered, and in 1789, enfeebled and sixty-three, he set out for his last journey through Europe to Russia. His name was widely known and honoured ; this at least is to the credit of the powers of his day that they threw every prison open to him, and welcomed his suggestions ; and the influence of his reputation and personality on the objects of his solicitude was such that he once quelled, unarmed and alone, a riot of several hundred prisoners who had murdered their jailers. At the close of 1789 he had reached Kherson, in Russian Tartary, where he wished to inspect the military hospitals, Russia and Turkey being at war. He had sighed occasionally for a peaceful old age in Buckinghamshire ; he died in a Russian village, and his remains were followed to the grave " by some two or three thousand spectators, an escort of cavalry, and a crowd of carriages, including the sumptuous equipage of the Prince of Moldavia, drawn by six horses covered with scarlet cloth." In Stepanovka, a white pyramid stands over his grave. In St. Paul's Cathedral is his statue. It was the first to be placed there, and represents him " in a classic costume, with shock hair, broken shackles at his feet, and a key in his right hand," and rustics are reported to have mistaken it for an effigy of St. Peter. That career and that statue may be taken as representing symbolically the relation between life and art in the eighteenth century. They loved, feared, and broke their hearts ; but it didn't strike them to put it into their poetry. They adventured and died like men : and, commemorating their heroes, they reduced the most extraordinary of careers to a marble toga and a couple of dead metaphors. That is the worst of too unmitigated a reign of " taste " : but it has its charms, and nobody has ever appreciated them more exquisitely than Mr. Austin Dobson.

# MR. GEORGE MOORE'S TAPESTRY

SOME years ago Mr. George Moore, determined no longer to court the insults of the library censorship, announced his intention of having his future books privately printed and issued to subscribers. The new era has seen the production of several books very agreeable in physical appearance and very diverse in character. " The Brook Kerith " was followed by " A Story-Teller's Holiday," in which one delicious and beautiful tale was surrounded by others which had little point beyond their grossness, and that by " Avowals," one of the most original and companionable of his books. A play came next, and now we have a novel on a large scale, in which he has retold a classic story of love. He is nothing if not enterprising ; who would have thought to hear him talking mediæval history and even sprinkling his pages with " alacks," " withals," and " twains " ? His scene is Paris in the early twelfth century, when Nominalists and Realists were dividing the world of thought, and the bold and brilliant young philosopher Abélard was acquiring an influence which alarmed the clergy. He meets Héloise, a girl fresh from a convent, living with her uncle, a Canon of Nôtre Dame. As Paolo and Francesca came together over their book, so these two do over Virgil and Ovid, and the Chanson de Roland. They elope. They part, after Héloise has conceived, because she wishes him to enter the Church, where alone a career is open to a philosopher as great as Plato. The uncle insists on a secret marriage ; there is a disingenuous renouncement of wedlock in order that Abélard may realise his ambitions, which do not stop short of the Papacy ; Héloise goes into a nunnery, consoled at times by the presence of her son, who has the remarkable name of Astrolabe : she waits for Abélard for nine years : she then hears how long ago her uncle had him seized and mutilated ; they meet for the last time ; and they separate to know no more of each other except through letters. That is Mr. Moore's outline. How has he filled it in ?

Meditating on Mr. Moore's book, one realises that several sorts of great novel might have been made out of his theme and his period, and that hints of them all are to be found in his book. The relics of the twelfth century are not so profuse as those of the fifteenth ; there is a certain lack of materials for the construction of a vivid picture of life, at any rate, in the towns. It isn't that a few anachronisms matter ; I, for one, had Mr. George Moore mentioned artichokes, should not have gone to a book of reference to see if artichokes had been introduced into France at that date. Yet a novelist cannot put down things that he knows to be absurd and that the reader will know to be absurd ; while years of *ad hoc* research are apt to deaden the creative impulse and result in a catalogue. Still, a man's imagination might be captured by that period, and form a bright and detailed picture of its physical aspects and spiritual movements. " Ivanhoe " and " The Cloister and the Hearth " were worth writing. Any good picaresque novel, again, is a fine thing to write ; a novel, whatever its period, in which the central personage or group passes through a variety of amusing or romantic scenes, and encounters a variety of strange people, each with his peculiar habits and his store of tales ; a " Lavengro" of the twelfth century, well done, would be worth having. Finally, the story of Abélard and Héloise, passionate and unfortunate lovers, with the added interest of being very intelligent, might make one of the most moving books in the world.

Beyond doubt a great novel is conceivable which should have elements of all three. Mr. Moore's has. It is a blend, and the mingling is cunningly done, although there are places where his vagrant tendency gets a little too much the upper hand. But it is a pale blend. His gallant tapestry is well woven, of good quality, but faded. He does not give a full and convincing picture of the period, much as he talks of the Crusades and the Church, Nominalism and Realism, and studious though he is to mention troubadours and gleemen, lepers and wolves. These are mentioned, but as a rule they are not clearly seen or in their force felt. No swarming scene of action remains in one's memory after one has read the novel : even Paris and its priests and students is visualised only dimly and in fragments ; the crowds make no noise, and we are not even sure about the architecture. The wandering part of the story, again, lacks humour, colour, and character. Abélard and Héloise, with the servant Madelon, make a long journey together, by forest roads to Orleans, by boat to Nantes. Abélard makes another, first alone, and then in company with his old master, a ruined Count. A large part of France is traversed ;

the travellers sleep in inns and houses and woods ; they encounter all weathers, see many birds and beasts and flowers ; they converse with each other, and strike many companions of the road, gleemen, pedlars, and pardoners. Everybody, too, tells stories faintly reminiscent of the " Fabliaux " and the " Cent Nouvelles Nouvelles," not to mention the " Heptameron." That the discursive method suits Mr. Moore nobody who has read his volumes of memoirs needs to be told. But he has not succeeded here. His publicans and pardoners have not the life of his Edward Martyns and A. E.s ; his suns do not burn and his rains do not drench ; his landscapes are not differentiated ; and his embedded anecdotes, though conducted with very great skill, lack the last degree of—well, punch—the author's interest in them apparently warming only on the few occasions on which, in these volumes, he permits himself to be disgusting. There are amusing and beautiful patches, but the whole is dullish. And with what is after all his main concern, the amours of Abélard and Eloisa, he cannot be held to have perfectly succeeded. There are two principal reasons for this. One is that he has imperfectly drawn, if not imperfectly apprehended, the character of Abélard, who is not merely a puzzle, but a puzzle which does not excite us to solution. His Abélard only interests us because Héloise is interested in him, and seldom at that ; even when the worst calamities befall him we do not much mind ; here, as often in Mr. Moore's books, one feels that the author's women characters attract him more than his men.

# MR. GEORGE MOORE'S TAPESTRY

But another reason of the love-story's failure to hold us is that there is an inadequate stress laid upon the more significant parts of it. Now and again there are sentences of a tender beauty and analytic passages of some subtlety, but passion, if often referred to, is never made fully evident. The crises of emotion are not communicated to the reader ; over everything Mr. Moore ambles smoothly on ; the tone of the sentences does not vary, whatever their content ; one thing comes after another and we turn the pages with unruffled equanimity. So it comes to pass that, reading again what should be one of the powerfully affecting of all the true stories in the world, one is very seldom conscious of the faintest wing-touch of suffering, we are infinitely less grieved and elated than we have been by the mere fairy-tale of " Aucassin and Nicolette." It is a half-realised tale of old unhappy far-off things ; the age and the distance are more noticeable than the unhappiness ; it is stretched out to thinness. The inadequacy of Mr. Moore's treatment is all the more annoying because his invention of incident has not failed. Time after time he brings us to a place where he might have written a memorable page, and always he skims over the great moment in a polished conversational way. One does not ask him to " lay it on too thick " ; but restraint is one thing, and the apparent absence of anything to restrain is another.

Were the book written by anyone but a man of genius, I should not have elaborated the case against it like that. I do not wish to convey the impression that it sent me to sleep, or to suggest that it has not great merits. Héloise frequently comes to life. There are delightful scenes in her uncle's house at Paris, and again in the convent to which she retires, after losing her husband ; and intermittently we feel her pangs : above all, during those long years of separation, when she did not even know where Abélard, immured above the grey sea of Brittany, was, and talked absent-mindedly to the nuns, was troubled about her child, and woke from restless sleep to " sit up in bed scared, watching the grey window pane." Some of the minor characters, especially the fat and selfish Canon, are well done ; there is grace and interest in certain of the disquisitions on theology and metaphysics ; and above all, there is Mr. Moore's prose style. The book may be monotonously written, but so high a level of monotony has never been reached. We may sometimes miss the right word, but we are never acutely conscious of the wrong one. By long labour Mr. Moore has arrived at a simplicity of diction and phrase which is a true simplicity ; he has discovered his natural method of expression and shed the acquired ; every sentence comes easily and flows into the next ; it is a stream of perfect talk. Even the least arresting and most rambling of his pages is unmistakably the work of an artist in prose and may arouse envy by virtue of its easy elegance of movement and purity of language.

And it would be absurd not to add a tribute to the energy, witness of a rare devotion to his art, which produced a book so elaborate and so ambitious when the author has reached an age at which most novelists are content to make dabbling efforts to repeat their former successes. It is the biggest job Mr. Moore has ever attempted to tackle, and the very great labour of its composition must have been preceded and accompanied by a considerable labour of research. Failure though the book may be, one instinctively judges it by the highest standards. And it leaves me with the feeling that Mr. Moore's best book may be yet to come, so active is still his mind and so unquenched his desire to excel his feats of craftsmanship. But if it does come I suspect that it will not be a book with a great theme appealing to the deeper feelings, but the book of a raconteur, an audacious humorist, a connoisseur in art, nature, and the emotions, a man who by this time ought to know himself more akin to Boccaccio and Watteau than to Shakespeare or Dickens. One cannot help admiring the perverse pride of one who continues in a wish to do something which he has not done before, but Mr. Moore was not made to be a great romantic writer. Happily he discovered long ago that he was made for something better than a " realistic " writer.

# ANDREW MARVELL

THE city of Hull is to celebrate the tercentenary of the birth of Andrew Marvell, who represented Hull in Parliament from 1659 till his death in 1678. Marvell was a son of the Rev. Andrew Marvell, rector of Winestead, who became master of the Hull Grammar School in 1624. The younger Andrew was taught by his father, went to Cambridge in 1633 as a Sizar of Trinity, and in 1638 was admitted a Scholar. In 1641, or thereabouts, he went off for a four years' tour on the Continent. He seems during the early portion of the Civil War to have mixed in Royalist circles ; but the temper which inspired his famous eulogy of Charles I on the scaffold, embedded in a congratulatory ode to Cromwell, saved him from discomfort without involving him in dishonour. From 1650 till 1652 he was tutor to Fairfax's daughter Mary at the General's country seat, and in the latter year he was recommended by Milton (who had gone blind) as assistant Latin (Foreign) Secretary. He obtained the position in 1657. Next year we hear of his being given six yards of mourning on Cromwell's death ; in 1659 he was elected member for Hull; on the Restoration in 1660 he not merely did not suffer because of his support of the Protector, but was largely instrumental, by vigorous lobbying, in saving Milton from Tyburn or the gaol. In 1663 he went with Lord Carlisle on a mission to Scandinavia and Russia ; he published several political and religious tracts ; and he died in 1678.

# ANDREW MARVELL

Certain of his verses had come out as pamphlets. The more polemic of them had to wait. But he left a widow of whom the one thing we know is that she at once set herself after his death to collect all his non-satirical poems. They came out in 1681, in a folio with a portrait. Verses of another kind were at last printed and attributed to him in the " State Poems " in William's reign, and in 1726 Thomas Cooke published a two-volume collection. But it is not to Cooke that Grosart and Aitken, Marvell's latest editors, have looked for authority. The basic edition of Marvell was that produced in 1776 by a collateral descendant, Captain Thompson. This useful and enthusiastic mariner had a manuscript book containing several fine unpublished poems, and he printed, besides the poems, Marvell's correspondence with the Hull Corporation, and also his prose writings. We have in the history of Marvell's works a story in which his city may rightly pride itself. For both Thompson, Marvell's first important editor, and Aitken, his last, were Hull men. But the Mayor and Corporation of 1670 would be surprised could they hear that their cheerful little red-faced member is chiefly remembered as a delicate lyrist.

Most of Marvell's best poems were, it is supposed, written before the Restoration—many of them while he was tutor to Fairfax's daughter. Almost all are in octosyllabic couplets, a kind of verse in which, at his best, he is excelled by no English poet. " Where the remote Bermudas ride " is a poem perfect in form and unique in kind : as a rule he was best when in a garden or a meadow, or writing light pastoral dialogues or tender epitaphs.

Everybody knows the garden poem containing the lines :

> Annihilating all that's made
> To a green thought in a green shade,

lines which precede two of the loveliest and most dexterously simple stanzas in all literature. But the gardens are all over his book. The whole of the long poem " Upon Appleton House " is full of the scent of flowers, and the fertility of his light fancy was inexhaustible. Take this description of a soldier's garden as a model of extreme artificiality which is not allowed to smother reality :

> See how the flowers, as at parade,
> Under their colours stand displayed ;
> Each regiment in order grows,
> That of the tulip, pink, and rose.
> But when the vigilant patrol·
> Of stars walks round about the pole,
> Their leaves that to the stalks are curled
> Seem to their staves the ensigns furled.
> Then in some flower's belovèd hut,
> Each bee, as sentinel, is shut,
> And sleeps so, too, but, if once stirred,
> She runs you through, nor asks the word.

His rhythms are as smooth as possible, and he will go for many lines without inversions, in a sort of inspired conversational way. And his nature was not conventional nature. He saw things for himself. Lines like—

> And through the hazels thick espy
> The hatching throstle's shining eye,

which are rare in our Caroline poetry, are common in Marvell. The marks of his period are to be found in occasional conceits and tropes. Having been communing with birds and plants, he has grown so close to them that he says :

> Give me but wings as they ; and I
> Straight floating on the air shall fly ;
> Or turn me but, and you shall see
> I was but an inverted tree.

Describing a hospital mansion that has no architectural grandeur, he ventures :

> A stately frontispiece of poor
> Adorns without the open door ;
> Nor less the rooms within commends
> Daily new furniture of friends.

This was of the time, but more frequently Marvell reminds us of a later time. " The Picture of Little T. C. in a Prospect of Flowers " has often been compared to the similar composition of Prior. In many descriptive passages we are reminded of Gay at his best. For example :

> Oh, what a pleasure 'tis to hedge
> My temples here with heavy sedge ;
> Abandoning my lazy side,
> Stretched as a bank into the tide ;
> Or to suspend my sliding foot
> On the osier's underminéd root,
> And in its branches tough to hang
> While at my line the fishes twang.

There is very little passion in his poetry, but much affection : no majesty, but much grace. Innocence and Quiet were his Muses ; looking both at fields and at people he reaped " the harvest of a quiet eye." His is pastoral poetry before it hardens into conventionalism. His nymphs are still real people, his fishes are not yet finny tribes, nor his woods groves. When he commends a maiden there is a sufficient tinge of genuineness in the commendation. And he does it as exquisitely as it can be done. There is she who—

> Counts her beauty to converse
> In all the languages as hers ;
> Nor yet in those herself employs,
> But for the wisdom, not the noise ;
> Nor yet that wisdom would affect,
> But as 'tis Heaven's dialect.

And she of whom he wrote :

> Her soul was on Heaven so bent,
> No minute but it came and went ;
> That, ready her last debt to pay,
> She summed her life up every day ;
> Modest as morn, as mid-day bright,
> Gentle as evening, cool as night :
> 'Tis true ; but all too weakly said ;
> 'Twas more significant, she's dead.

And the sweetest of all is the nymph, not directly described, who laments her little pale fawn shot by passing troopers :

# ANDREW MARVELL

> Thou ne'er didst alive
> Them any harm, alas ! nor could
> Thy death yet do them any good.
> I'm sure I never wished them ill ;
> Nor do I for all this, nor will.

That is a characteristic passage from the member
for Hull. But he had another aspect : as a satirist
he vied with Oldham, if not with Dryden.

If Marvell, in his serious poems, is a bridge between the mid-seventeenth century and the age of
Gay and Prior, his satirical poems are also transi-
tional. They are almost all in couplets. The earliest,
choked and rambling and stumbling, are clearly
under the influence of Donne ; the latest, such as
" Nostradamus' Prophecy," anticipate the smooth
closed epigrammatic verses of the Augustans. Some
interest in the details of political history is needed
for a man to read Marvell's Satires all through.
Most of them—privately circulated in MS. during
his lifetime and not " released for publication "
until the Glorious Revolution—were satires upon
the corruption and debauchery of Charles II, his
brother and their satellites at Court and in Parliament. The purity of the writer's motives is never
in doubt. The reader never feels, as he must when
perusing the works of many such men, that the
author would rather flagellate anybody than nobody.
He was concerned for the State and, as a monarchist,
he let the King down as lightly as he could. He
seldom went farther, when in the King's person,
than where, in the dialogue between Charles I's
horse at Whitehall and Charles II's at Woolchurch,
he makes the latter say :

De Witt and Cromwell had each a brave soul ;
I freely declare it, I am for old Noll ;
Though his government did a tyrant resemble,
He made England great and his enemies tremble.

But the purity of his motives and the soundness of
his judgment regarding individuals do not make his
satires uniformly readable, and it was only intermittently that he achieved in them the triumphs of
art which will keep even purely topical satire alive.
He who cares to read them, however, will continually be rewarded by sharp little witticisms and
gleams of warm and gentle humour. In the earliest
of all we find the youth who is deserted by his hired
poet :

Who should commend his mistress now ?  Or who
Praise him ?  Both difficult indeed to do
With truth.

" The Character of Holland " is a beautiful example
of deliberately farcical hyperbole. " Holland, that
scarce deserves the name of land " gives the key-
note. It is formed by the off-scouring of the coasts
of Briton, which the Dutch have laboriously heaped
together, " Building their watery Babel far more
high To reach the sea, than those to scale the sky ! "

Glad then, as miners that have found the ore,
They, with mad labour fished the land to shore,
And dived as desperately for each piece
Of earth, as if it had been of ambergris,

## ANDREW MARVELL

Collecting anxiously small loads of clay,
Less than what building swallows bear away,
Or than those pills which sordid beetles roll,
Transfusing into them their dunghill soul.

Of his later works, the most considerable take the
then popular form of " Instructions to a Painter " :
telling the artist what to paint, the poet described
everything in society and politics to which he
objected. All of these works were anonymous ; but
some of Marvell's controversial prose was acknowledged. His greatest success was with his " Re-
hearsal Transposed," in which he attacked Samuel
Parker, who had claimed for princes the power to
determine their subjects' religion. Marvell's controversial wit was so good that when Roger l'Estrange,
the licenser, wanted to suppress it, the King himself (who would forgive anything provided it were
wittily done) told l'Estrange that he must not in-
terfere with it.

Marvell, the politician, was an incorruptible man
in a corrupt age. He cared for his country ; his
opinions were not coloured by ambition or personal
prejudice. He took his Parliamentary duties so
seriously that he wrote to his constituents daily,
they recognising his solicitude with a regular salary
and frequent presents of barrels of beer. Yet it may
be doubted whether he had much influence on the
course of events, and I cannot think that those who
have commended his abandonment of poetry for
the public service have come anywhere near proving
that he did wisely. They are thinking rather of a
hypothetical than of the real case. Marvell did not

hold high office, and he seldom spoke in the House : few, probably, took the slightest notice of his admirable example of incompatibility; and if, through his entrance into politics, we lost a few lyric poems equal to his best, we have, I imagine, lost more than his contemporaries gained.

Marvell seems to have been, one may conclude by saying, as sensible a critic as he was a politician. He recognised immediately the " might " and " majesty " of " Paradise Lost," and the nature of Butler's subject did not prevent him from paying several handsome tributes to " Hudibras." In every capacity Marvell had not merely the desire, but the ability, to be both honest and fair.

# A DICTIONARY

LEARNING and the desire and capacity for research do not always go with a zest for life. Many of our standard works are far drier than they have any reason to be. Take Webster's " Dictionary," for instance. It is beyond all doubt the best dictionary of its size and scope in existence ; if one cannot have the great Oxford compilation, Webster is the next best thing. But Noah Webster and his successors, for all their magnificent devotion to their task, have not got much colour into their work. It was not always so. Cotgrave's definitions were full of salt, and Dr. Johnson deliberately made his work at once as accurate and as entertaining as he could. Modern lexicographers have feared the reproach of superficiality and have excluded personality from their work. It is a very great pleasure therefore to get *An Etymological Dictionary of Modern English* from Mr. Ernest Weekley.

One knows from experience that Mr. Weekley would contrive to avoid unnecessary dullness even if he were compiling a railway guide ; but that he would also get the trains right. This dictionary is not meant to be a substitute for Webster and his kind, but a complement to them. Mr. Weekley's aim is to cover our " literary and colloquial vocabulary, so far as the former is not purely archaic and the latter not purely technical or local " ; he excludes most modern scientific terms, and endeavours to include current slang words, many of which have been overlooked by his predecessors, and all foreign words which are likely to occur in reading and educated conversation. He has picked and chosen his ground, and frankly admits it. But another thing he admits without shame is that he has done his best to make his learning palatable.

Mr. Weekley, to some extent in his definitions and to a large extent in his illustrations, has returned to the Johnson tradition, his affection for which is displayed in his reproduction of Johnson's best things. "It has always seemed to the compiler," he says, "that a dictionary without quotations is too unrelieved in its austerity. Those included here range chronologically from the Venerable Bede to Mr. Horatio Bottomley." The result is something which is not merely a dictionary, but an anthology ; a book, even, which one might without brutality leave lying about in one's visitors' bedrooms. He does not, any more than Johnson did, take pains to secure the presence of at least one facetious remark on every page, but when the spirit moves him he puts down a definition which lays bare some small portion of his intellectual history. This is what he says, for instance, about " unquestionably " :

In philology usu. in refer. to some hazy recollection of an amateur theory propounded in the " correspondence column."

He supports this with two quotations from newspapers. One goes : " ' Odds ' is unquestionably a corruption of ' orts,' " which appeared in the *Daily Chronicle*, and the other is a similarly bold sentence from the *Observer*. Like Johnson, he does not

A DICTIONARY

disdain to put in clear references to his own experiences. One illustration, he feels, will do as well as another ; so why not choose illustrations which will give the reader a little amusement when he strays upon them ? Hence we get, under " Nietzscheism," some extremely uncomplimentary remarks made by a monthly paper on Professor Weekley himself ; and under " monger " we find :

> Common since 16 cent. in nonce-formations implying " one who carries on a contemptible or discreditable ' trade ' or ' traffic ' in what is denoted by the first element of the compound." (N.E.D.).
> Professor Weekley is well known to our readers as the most entertaining of living word-mongers. —(*Daily News*, November 8, 1916.)

" Values " is illustrated by only two quotations, which together make a poignant short story. These are they :

> We apologise to Mr. Wells for using the word " values " since he dislikes it.—(*Times Lit. Supp.*, June 5, 1919.)
> The hooligan sees none of the values of the stranger.—(H. G. Wells, *Observer*, January 18, 1920.)

and under " conscience " stands the following quotation :

> A conscientious objector, who gave an address at Knutsford, was fined £4 at Warrington for defrauding the railway company.—(*Daily Chronicle*, April 24, 1918.)

# BOOKS REVIEWED

Throughout he has studied, even when not (so to speak) parading an *arrière-pensée*, as he does here, to make his quotations lively. He has illustrated " verisimilitude " with the best of all possible quotations : Pooh-Bah's " Corroborative detail intended to give artistic verisimilitude to a bald and unconvincing narrative." Under " vengeance " we find an extract from the *Observer* : " A distinguished neutral calls it peace with a vengeance." " Mixed metaphor " is exemplified with a remarkable quotation from the *Fortnightly* for July, 1919 :

> In 1914 our old, regular army crossed swords with a great numerical superiority of the cream of the German host at concert pitch and undamaged by war.

This is much better than resuscitating once more Sir Boyle Roche's rat, which was floating in the air and should be nipped in the bud. Of all these striking illustrations, one of the most surprising comes on the very first page. It illustrates the colloquial use of " A.1," and runs :

> A proper A.1 copper-bottom lie.

Would you believe that that comes out of *The Times* of 1917 ? In its solemn context it comes with almost as much unexpectedness as the quotation which stands alone in its glory beneath the long dissertation on the word " German " :

> He called me a German and other filthy names. (Defendant in Middlesex Police Court, 1915.)

# A DICTIONARY

Much knowledge may be acquired by anyone who studies Professor Weekley's less topical quotations. Looking up " Panjandrum," I learn (I at least did not know it before) that the celebrated rigmarole about " What ! No Soap ? " was written by Foote. Underneath it is Panopticon, a word which was coined by Bentham " as name for ideal circular prison in which captives could be always watched." Whether the great Utilitarian thought that this invention would promote the greatest happiness of the greatest, or any, number is not recorded ; but Professor Weekley's phrase leads one to reflect on the beautiful elasticity of the word " ideal." I strolled from this, by a natural progress, to " Utilitarian." This word apparently has been traced back not to any philosophic work, but to Galt's " Annals of the Parish." Under " fountain-pen " we find surprisingly early references, as for instance one in an advertisement printed in the *Morning Chronicle* of June 11, 1788 : " Portable fountain pens to carry ink and write well, made and sold by E. T. Williams, No. 13, Strand." " Portmanteau word " was invented by Lewis Carroll : examples given include " Eurasian," " Bakerloo," " electrocute," " squarson," and " gerrymander " : the thing was older than the name for it. Two other oddities I must quote. Professor Weekley has been so lucky as to find in a work of Queen Anne's own time a passage which shows that the sentence by which Queen Anne chiefly lives was older than she. Swift, in his " Polite Conversation," has this dialogue :

" What news, Mr. Neverout ? Why, Madam, Queen Elizabeth's dead."

And under the word, new to myself, " mugger " I find this chaste entry :

> MUGGER. Broad-nosed Indian crocodile. Hind. " magar." Curiously confused in quotation below with " nuzzer," ceremonial present.
>
> Sir Salar Jung was presented to the Queen and offered his mugger as a token of allegiance, which her Majesty touched and restored.

Even Queen Victoria might have been for a moment at a loss if it really had been a broad-nosed crocodile.

Most of the latest slang is to be found in Professor Weekley's book. Many words which became popular during the war were older than the war. " Cushy " probably came from the East, and " is said to be Hind. from Pers. *khush*, pleasure." " Wangle," one of the words for the use of which occasion is most frequently found nowadays, is stated to have been recorded as printers' slang in 1888 ; and it has been found in a book by Mr. Edgar Wallace, published two years before the war. " Fed up," as most people will remember, first became popular at the time of the South African War, but Mr. Weekley produces an example older than that from G. W. Steevens's book, " With Kitchener to Khartoum." Of another interesting and popular phrase he observes : " Mod. ' to get it in the neck ' appears to allude to ' where the chicken got the axe.' A further playful variation is ' where Maggie wore the beads.' " " Scrap " is far older than most people would think. A sentence of 1679-80 runs : " They are in great fear Sir Robt. Payton should bring them into yᵉ scrappe." On many other colloquial terms light is shed. " Thorough-paced," which is now never used save in a derogatory connection, was once a quite straightforward word, and men spoke of " a thorough-paced Christian." " Rhino," as one of the hundred synonyms for money, is traced to the seventeenth century, and is " apparently connected by some obscure joke with ' rhinoceros,' as ' rhinocerical,' wealthy, also occurs." " Loafer " is referred to as a newly-invented Yankee word in Dana's "Two Years Before the Mast" (1840), and " bally " is traced back to 1885, where its origins are matter of speculation. The verb " to bitch," used as an equivalent of to bungle or make a mess of it, is described as " thinned form of ' botch.' " Under " blimy " one searches in vain for the results of research, the Professor being content with : " For Gawblimy, God blind me ; cf. swop me bob." Of modern terms of derision, " cad " is said to have an Oxford origin, and " bounder " and " rotter " to have started on their careers from Cambridge. In my time their equivalent at the latter University was usually " tout," now perhaps fallen into disuse, and absent (in this sense) from Professor Weekley's Dictionary.

I do not affect to have read this book right through, though its charms have beguiled me into reading twenty times more of it than the minimum amount which would have made me capable of writing a thoroughly deceptive review. But I have noticed several omissions which can scarcely have been deliberate. No man making a particular effort to embody the whole of contemporary slang should

have overlooked the verb " to jaw " with its schoolboy derivative, now respectably established, " pi-
jaw." Professor Weekley gives " wind up," but
misses " cold feet," and his sporting vocabulary
does not include the common cricketing term
" rabbit." Had he carried his researches into the
more adventurous spheres of finance he might have
heard the term " put the hooks into," and also
" cough up," neither of which he records. However, most of the terms by which I have tested him
are here, and he seems to have made very few errors
which can be detected by a non-philologist. But he
has, I think, gone badly off the rails (there is another
metaphorical usage which he has missed) in dealing
with the word " profiteer." He thinks it a war-word
and ascribes to it the definite date 1915. But it was
current in the Labour movement for years before
the war, and I fancy that a search of the files of the
*New Age* might lead him to its origin.

# QUEEN VICTORIA

W HAT, could she read his book, would
Queen Victoria say of Mr. Lytton Strachey?
She would certainly think him a monster. She might
say that, like the pioneers of " Women's Rights,"
he deserved " a whipping " ; she might be tempted
to use phrases such as she used about the Russians :
" It makes the Queen's blood boil ! Oh, if the Queen
were a man, she would like to go and give those
Russians, whose word one cannot believe, a beat-
ing." But her judgments of strangers were frequently
hasty ; she was tempted to be deceived by surface
appearances : the slightest sign of a divagation from
her own opinion was liable to draw from her a
passionate demand for hostilities. And if she, or
anyone else, were deceived by appearances into
thinking Mr. Strachey's book anything but a tribute,
a great mistake would be made.

It was observed when Mr. Strachey wrote his
last book that he was, although a rather sceptical
and studiously ironical writer, a man anxious to be
just and capable of warm sympathy with certain
kinds of character. He has little use for the ordinary humdrum man. He regards the appellation
" Christian gentleman " as almost equivalent to a
term of reproach ; when he encounters the common, cautious, dutiful person he shoots one con-
temptuous bullet at him and leaves him for dead.
But he can admire : he admired, within limits,
General Gordon, Cardinal Newman, and Florence
Nightingale. He likes, understands, and respects

adventurousness, recklessness, passionate sincerity in any form, even discontent, because it does not go with smugness ; and by the same token he is attracted by, and in effect extols, Queen Victoria. " It was," he says, " her sincerity which gave her at once her impressiveness, her charm, and her absurdity."

In 300 pages he gives a picture of her whole life ; as girl (so guarded that she was never left alone in a room with a single person), as young monarch (coming like " the spring " after her debauched uncles), as happily married woman, as cloistered and laborious widow, and as the aged Empress who was almost a legendary figure whilst she was still alive, and enjoyed an Indian summer of mellow glory. Throughout he is never—he never would be —tempted to sentimentalise. He attributes to her nothing that she does not possess. He never disguises the fact that her speech was usually emotional gush, that she had little intellect, that her interferences in public affairs were uninformed, and might have been disastrous. He is, in opinion, as opposed to Queen Victoria as he could be ; she had probably not a notion about this world or the next, the throne, the hearth, or the altar, which he shares. But she was honest and she was fiery ; she knew what she wanted and fought for what she wanted ; she slaved at what she conceived to be her duty, and she had a great capacity for suffering ; she loved life and hated dying ; and her biographer cannot but be drawn to her. She was a powerful, a puzzling, and (whatever her pride and egoism) an attractive and affectionate woman. She is displayed as such here, but she would probably fly off at a tangent before discovering it. She had an acute nostril for *lèse-majesté*.

But here she is. Most of the materials are the old ones. Mr. Strachey has availed himself of a certain amount of private information, and he has seen the unpublished parts of Greville—which, by the way, might just as well be published at this date. But these new sources are comparatively unimportant. Everything depends on the perceptions and the art of the biographer. With all the old materials Mr. Strachey has given us a new picture of the Queen, and a new and (since he discovered a strain of dissatisfaction and melancholy in him) sympathetic portrait of Prince Albert.

The volume is an important addition to historical literature. The age appears as a background to the two central figures ; it is a century seen through a diminishing glass. And how clearly and amusingly seen ! Nobody who read " Eminent Victorians " will need to be told that Mr. Strachey's book is delightful reading. He has learnt his art, not from the historians and biographers, but from the artists. We are conscious, though not disagreeably conscious, throughout that he is taking his job seriously from an æsthetic, as well as from a historical, point of view ; that he is, in a general way, solicitous about proportion and in detail careful to select the significant episode and the significant characteristic and to order his words in the most telling way. There is no such short biography in English ; thinking of its analogues, one finds oneself inevitably comparing it not with records of fact, but with fictions. He is

really one of the post-Flaubert novelists. His work
is as uniform, as coherent, as economical as the best
short stories of Maupassant and Tchekov. Such
closeness and evenness of texture, such clarity and
terseness of phrase, can be found nowhere in biography. The book recalls rather such novels as
Couperus's "Old People and Things that Pass"—
though I am far from suggesting that Queen Victoria
and her Consort bore any resemblance to the central
characters of that very alarming study. And Mr.
Strachey, writing a short and sparsely-documented
book, in which years are often skimmed in a sentence, produces an effect of completeness which is
seldom produced by the two-volume monuments
of the last generation. Reflecting on the old Queen's
death at Osborne he says :

> Perhaps her fading mind called up once more
> the shadows of the past to float before it, and re-
> traced, for the last time, the vanished visions of
> that long history—passing back and back, through
> the cloud of years, to older and ever older memo-
> ries—to the spring woods at Osborne, so full
> of primroses for Lord Beaconsfield—to Lord
> Palmerston's queer clothes and high demeanour,
> and Albert's face under the green lamp, and
> Albert's first stag at Balmoral, and Albert in his
> blue and silver uniform, and the Baron coming
> in through a doorway, and Lord M. dreaming at
> Windsor with the rooks cawing in the elm-trees,
> and the Archbishop of Canterbury on his knees
> in the dawn, and the old King's turkey-cock
> ejaculations, and Uncle Leopold's soft voice at

Claremont, and Lehzen with the globes, and her mother's feathers sweeping down towards her, and a great old repeater-watch of her father's in its tortoiseshell case, and a yellow rug, and some friendly flounces of sprigged muslin, and the trees and the grass at Kensington.

It is a long catalogue of the typical incidents of a long life. The point is that when they are thus drifted in series before us, we are already familiar with them all. In three hundred pages a whole century has been indicated ; and, turning back to a scene which one assumes must have occupied a chapter, one finds it suggested in a brief parenthesis.

Mr. Strachey's craft and assiduity have displayed before us the long and crowded life of his heroine, a succession of social changes, the crumbling of one era after another, and a swarm of minor characters. In retrospect one finds that his gift of selection has imprinted very many minor portraits on the memory. There are the seven sons of George III : the Regent with his stomach released from his stays, and the Duke of Kent with his precision and his debts, and King William, " A bursting, bubbling old gentle-man, with quarter-deck gestures, round rolling eyes, and a head like a pineapple," who went redder than usual when the King of the Belgians insisted on drinking water at his table. There is dear, absent-minded, wise, flippant old Lord Melbourne, " the autumn rose " of the eighteenth century, of whom Greville said that he was " a man with a capacity for loving without having anything in the world to love." There is the old Duke, with his shrewd eyes, his nose, and his wry smile, always called in at an emergency and summing up any position in a laconic sentence. There is Lord Palmerston, without principle, but holding that one really couldn't think of the Neapolitan prisons without getting angry ; volatile and wilful : turning up at Osborne just after the Consort's death " in the pink of health, brisk, with his whiskers freshly dyed, and dressed in a brown overcoat, light grey trousers, green gloves, and blue studs." There is Gladstone, just glimpsed but truly seen ; and Napoleon III, whose gipsyishness fascinated the Queen ; and Disraeli, actor in his own play, who laid the flattery on with a trowel, and received favours never bestowed on another subject. A few of these minor characters are less clear than others : the Duchess of Kent, Lehzen, and the conscientious Stockmar, who advised that the Prince of Wales should be " brought up in the creed of the Church of England " without being led to believe in " the supernatural doctrines of Christianity." But these are figures which should properly be less dim than those others : they are the mysterious outskirts. Generally speaking, the impression made is the impression of a consummately written short novel : each figure displayed in proportion to its importance in the story, each incident elaborated according to the degree and weight of its relevance to the main theme.

And Mr. Strachey's writing is almost consistently excellent. He wastes no words. He has, as has been remarked, his outlook ; and his irony is often crystallised in a sentence, even in a sentence unspoken. " And fortunately, if the world would not understand,

there were faithful friends who did. There
was Lord Granville, and there was ' kind Mr.
Theodore Martin '"; a chapter of criticism is implicit in the phrase. Describing the aptness of the
design of the Albert Memorial, which was modelled
on a form of shrine, he says, with brutal reticence,
that the architect's " idea was particularly appro-
priate, since it chanced that a similar conception,
though in the reverse order of magnitude, had
occurred to the Prince himself, who had designed
and executed several silver cruet-stands upon the
same model." The section on the Crimean War
begins with the uncannily adequate statement : " The
Crimean War brought new experiences, and most
of them were pleasant ones." Mr. Strachey never
sets up pointers to his jokes : he merely describes
a thing in very simple, but the right, words to get
his effects. We flow smoothly on from some merely
explanatory passage into sentences, equally matter-
of-fact on the surface, like these :

Upon the interior decorations Albert and
Victoria lavished all their care. The walls and the
floors were of pitch-pine, and covered with
specially manufactured tartans. The Balmoral
tartan, in red and grey, designed by the Prince,
and the Victorian tartan, with a white stripe,
designed by the Queen, were to be seen in every
room : there were tartan curtains, and tartan
chair-covers, and even tartan linoleums. Occasionally the Royal Stuart tartan appeared, for Her
Majesty always maintained that she was an ardent
Jacobite. Water-colour sketches by Victoria hung

93

upon the walls, together with innumerable stags'
antlers, and the head of a boar which had been
shot by Albert in Germany. In an alcove in the
hall stood a life-sized statue of Albert in Highland dress.

The quotations are as economically, as aptly, and
as gravely introduced ; for instance, this, which
stands without comment : " We were always in the
habit of conversing with the Highlanders—with
whom one comes so much in contact in the Highlands." Similarly, what it is misleading to call the
purple passages grow out of the context : they are
adequate, sometimes noble, but never obtruded.
Everything is interwoven, and in tone nothing stands
out. Mr. Strachey has really digested everything
he has taken in.

Victoria and Albert and their age are here recorded
as one man sees them. The picture cannot be final
or complete ; but it does present, and very clearly,
one aspect of the truth. Mr. Strachey has naturally
selected his facts in accordance with his temperament ; but he has not cheated, as a man making a
comic picture must be strongly tempted to do. And
whatever reservations and qualifications he may
have omitted, however others may differ from him
in the assessment of what people now call " relative
values," it is indisputable that so far as he goes he
is accurate, and that his portrait of his central figure
must, in its essentials, stand.

WILLIAM ERNEST HENLEY, whose collected works now appear, was born at Gloucester in 1849, and educated there. He was a man of large frame, but illness attacked him, and in 1873 he went to Edinburgh to seek the aid of Lister. For two years he was in hospital there, during which period he first met Stevenson, and conceived his " In Hospital " poems. Discharged as a permanent cripple and invalid, he edited *London* (1877-8), *The Magazine of Art* (1882-6), the *Scots (National) Observer* (1883-93), and the *New Review* (1893-8). He published many volumes of verse and criticism, and died in 1903 after celebrating the South African War, and causing considerable disturbance by a too drastic criticism of his dead friend Stevenson.

Henley, were he alive to-day, would be only seventy-two, but his reputation has already sustained strange vicissitudes. During his life-time he was known chiefly as a brilliant editor who had also the gift of forcible polemic writing and a peculiar power of attracting the affection and service of talented men. He certainly was a great editor. He thought, perhaps, too exclusively of what he was publishing and too little of the steps which might be taken to induce people to read it ; the consequence being that his contributors were the kernel of his public and all his papers were short-lived. But he knew a man of force when he met him, and most of the writers of his time, from Stevenson to Kipling, and from Kipling to Yeats, either established or enhanced their reputations in the pages which he edited. But an editor's reputation is a brief one. He may perform great services to literature in general and to particular authors, but no sooner has his last number appeared than his authors sail off on their own adventures, and his enterprise becomes a memory fading daily. No sooner had Henley died than the *National Observer* became a legend, to which ageing journalists referred with sentimental regret. The young noted the regret and were prepared to take the merit of the performance for granted ; they did not propose to go to the British Museum files in order to discover whether or not Henley was a great editor. That fame dwindled ; Henley became a " poet of the 'nineties," represented chiefly in anthologies by an apostrophe to England and " Out of the Night that covers me." Middle-aged gentlemen might still be met who were young men with Henley and talked of him as one who fascinated and permanently influenced them. But what had he left ? Certain verses. He was one of the lesser poets of the later Victorian age ; an energetic writer of verse who very occasionally rose to an almost accidental perfection. Yet it now seems probable that the poet in Henley will ultimately seem not the most important thing about him. If his name lives it will probably live as a critic ; and it may be that even yet some biographer may be tempted to investigate and immortalise him as a man.

A powerful and passionate personality, an enthusiasm for life and for literature, honesty, industry and faith are not in themselves sufficient to constitute a great, or even a good, poet. Henley had all

those attributes. We do not need the assertions of
his friends to convince us that he cared about letters,
took a devouring interest in men, individual and in
the mass, bore pain with gay courage, loved, hated,
and jested with vigour and gusto. All that can be
seen in his writings ; as also that tendency to shout
and to bully which so impressed his disciples, and
disseminated so widely the impression of his personality. All these things may be seen in his works,
but they are seen less purely in his poetry than elsewhere, and he lacked certain qualities which are
essential in verse if it is to make a deep or a lasting
appeal. Let it be admitted that now and then he
" pulled it off." But, generally speaking, he was,
when writing poetry, neither natural enough nor
careful enough. The horse-sense that marked much
of his criticism deserted him. He dispelled all un-
certainties in himself by loud vociferation. He lacked
the confidence to employ simple language ; he
attempted to carry the fort by storm and a plenitude
of great bombastic adjectives ; he could not state
precisely what he felt in language just adequate. It
was all very well, when he was sitting on his sofa,
beard bristling, hands swinging, eyes flashing, to
hammer away at his audience with his dogmas and
his denunciations. But a worked-up excitement is
no good in poetry; nor is the thin and padded
language of rapid dictation. Much of Henley's poetry
is precisely like dictated poetry. In a manner he
meant what he said. But he could not reflect and
labour until he had got accuracy. He must cover
the ground quickly. He must bang his notions into
the listener's head.

The result often was great expanses of cacophonous magniloquence that tire the ear and dazzle the eye. Is he describing ? We get :

Out of the poisonous East,
Over a continent of blight,
Like a maleficent Influence released
From the most squalid cellarage of hell,
The Wind-Fiend, the abominable—
The Hangman Wind that tortures temper and light—
Comes slouching, sullen and obscure,
Hard on the skirts of the embittered night ;
And in a cloud unclean
Of excremental humours, roused to strife
By the operation of some ruinous change,
Wherever his evil mandate rear and range,
Into a dire intensity of life,
A craftsman at his bench, he settles down
To the grim job of throttling London town.

Or is he exhorting, preaching his gospel of action ? Then we get (the starting-point being Lord Northcliffe's, then Mr. Alfred Harmsworth's, motor-car) :

Thus the Mercédes
Comes, O she comes,
This astonishing device,
This amazing Mercédes,
With Speed—
Speed in the Fear of the Lord.
So in the eye of the Lord,
Under the Feet of the Lord,

# HENLEY

Out of the measureless
Goodness and grace
In the Hand of the Lord.
Speed !
Speed on the Knees.
Speed in the Laugh,
Speed by the Gift,
Speed in the Trust of the Lord—
Speed.

It was meant. He believed. But not all the recapitu-
lations carry it home, nor all the copious capital
letters. His instrument was a coarse one, and his
hands, though strong, not delicate. He had too little
care about exactitude, either of meaning or of expression ; and too little ear. If his more ambitious
and robustious experiments in unrhymed verse
show this, so also do most of his attempts at quieter
song. The rhetorician becomes the jingler. The
excited apostle of vague but tremendous forces, the
booming chanter of " solemn ancientries " and
" plangent comforters " and a thousand other rather
too cumbersome things becomes a thin Heine, sing-
ing of dreams and roses with just too little compression and just too little music. We may explain
away much in him and his verse on the ground of
his lifelong pain. He, by temperament and physique
a man of action, compelled to inaction by his mala-
dies, naturally tended to glorify the Paradise from
which he had been shut out, to celebrate the grim
glories of war and adventure, speed and the sword,
to express himself through batterings and swirlings
of speech since his limbs would not do their work.

But he was not an artist in verse even when these tendencies were not operating. Except in a few places, merit is to be found in his poetry only when he is describing, with the vividness of good journalism, something he has seen, and, above all, when he is painting a portrait. The nurses, the doctors, the patients, in his Edinburgh hospital and the strange gallery of his London types : these remain in one's memory when the rest of his metrical writing has faded away. He had the eye of a Daumier or of a Phil May for the character in a face or a garment ; and he need not mention Rembrandt to assure us that the lighting of his hospital scenes was done by one who appreciated painting. His descriptions, moreover, are not merely external ; his characters are grasped inwardly, and his celebrated sonnet summary of Stevenson is only one out of several as good.

Yet most of these things are little more than rhymed—or, indeed, unrhymed !—prose. Little sensuous appeal is made to the ear ; the best word is not usually hunted for if the second best will roughly convey the idea ; that " spherical " form which is a quality of good poems is usually missing ; what we get is a series of energetic, interesting, and frequently picturesque statements. Henley's verse is commonly no more than the journalism of an unusual man ; he is at his best when he knows he is writing journalism. Some of the critical work now reprinted is careful and exhaustive ; the essay on Burns is deservedly famous. But much of it was casual, brief, hurried work ; and it is surprisingly good. Henley's prose was not always devoid of

affectations. He still would sometimes throw in an
unnecessarily resounding or archaic word ; he liked
parading his carefully-acquired knowledge of thieves'
slang ; he favoured unnecessary archaisms, such as
the use of " 'tis " for " it is." And the things he
says are still sometimes coloured too much by his
propagandist zeal : he bellows his revivalist doctrine
and looks menacingly round, prepared to thump
you on the head if you do not agree. But in a general
way he is far more natural in prose, and far more
subtle. His taste was good, his outlook was sane,
his intellect (when he would allow it) operated subtly,
he could discriminate even with his heroes, and his
heroes were invariably men. His reading was very
wide ; and his power, here, of compression was so
great that he could say many valuable and penetrating things, even in an article of a thousand words,
on one of the world's great masters. In the more
miscellaneous of these volumes there are very short
papers on Dickens and Rabelais, Gay, Congreve,
Fielding and Tolstoi, Richardson, Hood, Herrick
and Hugo ; and every one of them, though a mere
note, adds to one's information and assists one's
insight. And there is a beauty on Dumas. For there
Henley found an author who dreamed such men as
he would like to have been. His challenge to " whatever gods there be " may have been a little bombastic, not to say tautologous ; it may have savoured
a little of the whistle on a dark night to keep one's
spirits up and one's eyes from wandering into the
shadows. But he was a joyful and a gallant man. In
a generation which toyed with despair and disease
he would have none of either ; and his instinct for

character and for art was such that he made very few mistakes in judgment. The second and the fourth volumes of this edition are a most valuable contribution to literary history ; and they are amongst the most readable " books about books " that our age has produced.

The new edition is agreeable in appearance. The first volume includes several poems not previously reprinted from the papers in which they originally appeared. The plays which Henley wrote in collaboration with Stevenson are here ; they are vigorous, brisk, and vivid : the sort of plays that Mr. John Buchan might, but unfortunately does not, write. And it was a good idea to include with Henley's works the anthology he made, " Lyra Heroica." He is expressing himself here in the selection of poems by other men, and his spirit is better manifested in their poems than in his own. There is scarcely a thing in the book which is not at once gallant, chivalrous, and humane. There are aspects of life not represented in it and human needs which it does not satisfy. But so far as it goes it reflects as much credit on his character as it does on his taste and as much credit on his taste as it does on his scholarship. Every boy ought to be given it, and no man would be the worse for having it ; especially in a period like this, when the need for preserving one's ideals, one's cheerfulness, and one's determination to make the most of life under the shadow of death is more imperative than ever. I may add, just to provide a pleasing anti-climax, that a biographical introduction and a few notes would have been welcome in this edition.

# A CRITIC

JULES LEMAITRE, who died during the war, was amongst the first French writers of his time. But though he wrote stories, and stories of great charm, he was in the first instance a critic, not a professional novelist. The result is that during his lifetime he was in England almost completely unknown. Anatole France had been read here for a generation before a single book by the contemporary who was, in mind and manner, nearest to him had been translated. Mr. Evans has now, however, followed up his translation of Serenus with an admirable version of some of the essays in the eight volumes of Lemaître's "Les Contemporains."

Mr. Evans has made his selection wisely. He has chosen essays on subjects not too strange to the larger cultivated public. Anatole France, Bourget, Maupassant, Zola, Renan, Loti, Taine, George Sand, Bernhardt, de Sevigné, Joubert, Virgil, Thomas à Kempis : there is not one of these on whom a number of essays by Englishmen could not be found ; even Joubert has had his meed.

These papers, some of them very short, are as illuminating and delightful as any literary essays ever written. Lemaître was not primarily a propagandist of good but neglected literature, he was not (like Leigh Hunt) a standard-bearer of the promising young, and he was not (like Matthew Arnold) very concerned with moral causes. He took his subjects where he found them, often from among the acknowledged great. Anything that aroused his

curiosity did ; how did he react to " Boule-de-Suif,"
the " Mariage de Loti," or " Germinal " ; what
things in them attracted, amused, moved, or re-
pelled him ? That was what concerned him ; that
and the elegant transmission of his impressions. He
was avowedly preoccupied with description rather
than with judgment ; but the personality which
entered into his descriptions was a very peculiar
one, whimsical and tender, very acute of percep-
tion, masking a good deal of hankering under an
ironic exterior. He was eminently, in his scepticism,
a creature of his time ; but he was far more uncomfortable with it. Even when celebrating the
powers and reflecting the doubts of his contemporaries he often betrayed an implicit dislike of them.
Almost every reference to " this age " (*i.e.*, the last
age) : to its " stoic pessimism," its " ironical resig-
nation," its " strange mania for making out the
world very ugly and very brutal," reflects a regret
which he did not care to elaborate. He salutes Zola
as " an epic poet," but he did not end with the phrase
" a pessimist epic of human animalism " without
letting the reader see that he was more uncomfortable about it than Zola was. This clash of elements
in him made him unique among the critics of his
time ; he was of the company of Anatole France,
but his secret soul was with Joan of Arc. His writing
is always delicious ; natural, yet very precise, full
of odd turns, quiet, vivid, and admirably decked
with quotations. In retrospect it may be seen that
he was almost always right. . . .

" Oh, no," says Lemaître, " don't say I am right,
don't indeed ! " In his introduction, Mr. Evans

gives an account of Lemaître's and Anatole France's controversy with Brunetière as to the nature and objects of criticism. " To Brunetière's almost pathetic assertions that criticism to be of any value must be ' objective ' ; that the difference between a good work of art and a bad one could only be determined by reason and comparison, and that the critic must go by fixed standards, Anatole France replied by denying the possibility of ' objective ' criticism, smiling at reason, and flouting the fixity of any such critical standards." Lemaître said that his own method was simply to define and explain the impressions that he received from works of art :

When the impressionist critic has thus expounded his doctrine of universal relativity and has explained that, as he is imprisoned in his own personality, there is no standard to which he may refer his own opinions or those of others, he may be asked to state what then is the value of criticism. To this M. Lemaître replies that to become acquainted with the sensations aroused in another personality by reading a book that pleases is to prolong and intensify our own sensations.

" I assure you," said Lemaître, " it is possible for me, as for other people, to judge on principles and not on impressions. Only if I did so I should not be sincere. I should say things of which I should not be sure, whilst I am sure of my impressions." But is there nothing more that a critic can do unless he care to erect a body of artificial laws to which literature must conform, and insists that the unities must be preserved, " correctness " maintained, morality respected, immorality eschewed, and so forth ? Has he no alternative ? Must he choose between a renunciation of judgment and the claim to possess an infallible yard-measure of principle ?

Few men live thoroughly up to their theories, and behind Jules Lemaître's essays one can frequently trace the conviction that he is giving something more than a personal impression worth no more than any other personal impression. But the sceptical theory simply amounts to this : what is one man's meat is another man's poison, and everything in the world may be both meat and poison. " I think X is good, you think it is bad ; we cancel out." The position is certainly difficult to attack. But it does rather call to mind the flushed Freshman who has made his first stumble over the frontier of philosophy and takes up every casual assertion of knowledge with " How do you know you know anything ? " We may grant that we are in the dark about absolutes, and it is difficult to dispute about tastes. We may realise how standards change and how intelligent men differ. But a critic may, if he choose, still endeavour to make, without dishonesty, pronouncements which are something more than the records of personal impressions and judgments which are more than confessions of taste. Let us rule out the question of absolute validity ; the fact remains that mankind has been agreed in designating as the best literature that which has retained, humanly speaking, a permanent hold upon readers. It may quite easily be admitted that works with many great qualities may die young ; perhaps they serve an immediate purpose, strongly move a large body of contemporaries, but are crowded with ossifying topical references. It may be admitted, again, that to millions of people Mrs. Henry Wood was a greater writer than Mr. Meredith. Put in all the reservations. The fact remains that in the world in which critics live and for which they chiefly write the prime interest of a work of art lies in its chances of " lasting." Yes ; it may be taking the credit and letting the cash go. Also, as Anatole France is so often at pains to remark, the world will some day grow cold, and Homer and Mr. Garvice will lie in the same bed.

The source of our preoccupation here is as dark as everything else about us. But, under that mysterious and menacing cope we must have our toys, and we may amuse ourselves with admiring " immortal " literature as well as in any other way, and it *is* possible, without presumption and without dreaming of reaching infallible " principles," to escape to some extent the completely anarchistic and personal attitude of Jules Lemaître. A critic may, not too sternly, not with any hope of arriving at certainty, but with good hope of discovering some elements of truth and evolving " tests " of at least provisional value, regard literature from an historical and scientific point of view. Every reviewer who says " I do not think this book will last " is unconsciously referring to an opinion formed as a result of his study, however fragmentary that may have been, of the works of the past which actually have " lasted." Man's nature may change : the amœba was and the superman may be : and we feel little kinship with either. But if our historical epoch be isolated we may assemble literary facts and make deductions from them, just as any other kind of scientist does with facts of another kind. We may find that in a particular category of " lasting " works of art one or two nameable elements have always been present ; their absence in something professing to be a candidate for their company gives one ground for a judgment, if not for a judgment for which we can (or need) claim infallibility. There is, for instance, something more than a personal impression that " Dada poetry " (an extreme example) will not " live." Casually we all make this sort of judgment, with more or less of undeliberate investigation behind it. It might be made far more systematically ; works admitted to retain an active life after a hundred, or five hundred, years, may be set apart, sorted, analysed ; and most interesting and valuable results may flow from such a study, powerful weapons given to critics who do feel a little more need for dogmatising than was felt by M. Lemaître. . . .

All the same, I think we can, after all, leave it to the Germans to do the job thoroughly.

# MR. GOSSE'S CRITICISMS

MR. GOSSE'S *Books on the Table* is composed of weekly reviews contributed to a Sunday newspaper. It is as delightful and illuminating as any in the long series of its predecessors. Let us consider what this means.

When I had finished the book I sat down to reflect upon the limitations under which Mr. Gosse must work ; to imagine what it must be like to write a weekly column and a half about literature, with especial reference to new books. I think I have some dim apprehension of the difficulties of doing the work well at all, and especially of doing it in such a manner that one's articles shall be not merely readable after breakfast, when the newspaper reader has exhausted the political, the sporting and (possibly) the financial pages, but that they shall still have some savour, some appearance of value, when they are reprinted in book form. In the first place there must be (as I conjecture) the difficulty of a subject. Sometimes the subject is ready-made, as when a book of the quality of Mr. Gosse's own comes out, or some work like Mr. Lytton Strachey's, which the critic could not escape even if he would. But often enough a week must go by which sees the production of no book of surpassing, or even tolerable merit, and no book concerning any " literary figure " whose personality and powers provoke enthusiasm and curiosity. Beyond this difficulty there are the difficulties of Time and Space. On some prearranged day of the week, I suppose, a man in Mr. Gosse's position is expected to deliver his " copy." " Rarely, rarely comest thou, Spirit of Delight " is a complaint which has been echoed by all literary artists, but it would be precious little use saying it to an editor or a printer, especially over the telephone. The calendar must be obeyed, and I daresay that there are times when the day of delivery seems to recur with a malignant rapidity. And when the impulse does come it is at least conceivable that the prearranged amount of space may often seem very like a strait-waistcoat. Take the instance of a contemporary not yet sufficiently known to the public ; there must often be in the critic's mind an uncertainty as to whether to suppress necessary quotations from his author or comment by himself which he cannot but feel to be almost equally indispensable. All these suppositions, as I say, arose in mind when I contemplated Mr. Gosse's book. And I cannot but marvel that papers which, when I read them first, seemed to me excellent, and often very topical, journalistic columns should read now as though they had been composed at leisure and with a single eye to publication in a permanent form. Mr. Gosse has not split the difference between reviewing and criticism, journalism and literature ; he has abolished it.

It would be an impertinence at this time to call attention to the range of Mr. Gosse's erudition. In this volume he is equally at his ease with Ausonius and Mrs. Asquith, Guevara, Goethe, Mr. de la Mare, and Miss Daisy Ashford, and the index of persons and books to whom and which he makes reference fills ten closely-printed pages. Nevertheless he has no trace of that maddening habit—too common amongst people who know anything at all—of dragging in scraps of learning merely for the sake of showing that he possesses them. Learning is for use and for ornament, not for parrot-like repetition on parade, and the profoundest of literary critics have worn their knowledge most lightly. And when I say knowledge I do not mean that—although in some departments he is a specialist—Mr. Gosse knows more than any man living about Shakespeare's commas or the manuscripts of Dante. He is a scholar; but he is not primarily a scholar : he is a critic to whom the researches of scholars are useful material towards the formation of judgments on life and art ; he is a bibliographer and collector who does not take his pursuits with undue seriousness. He has spent a good deal of his life with an open book before him, but he has never lost sight of the relation between books and life.

This volume is naturally for the most part critical. Possibly the most signal of Mr. Gosse's gifts is his power of analysing the persons and describing the events that he has seen, but the portraits and the reminiscences in this volume are only incidental. Half his contents would be well described by his old title of " Gossip in a Library," half derives from a consideration of poems, essays, and " Lives " produced in our own time. Not novels. Mr. Gosse obstinately refuses to yield to the common delusion that the novel is necessarily the most important product of contemporary art, merely because the circulating libraries are chiefly stocked with it. He will deal with such novels as are really worth his

attention ; the mere " novel of the week " he looks
at with a blank stare. Literature in his hands never
loses its dignity ; but it must be confessed that
litterateurs sometimes lose theirs. For he belongs to
a race of critics commoner in France than here. He
never abandons himself to an author. He does not
look down on the tribes of men ; he stands a little
apart and examines them with shrewd and level
eyes. And even the greatest, thus considered by a
man who is not, however exquisite his æsthetic
appreciations, blinded by his ecstasies, are liable
to display certain asinine attributes. It is Mr. Gosse's
distinction that he can see and, for our delectation,
transcribe these without the slightest forgetfulness
of his main business, or the least risk of lampooning.

The whole time he knows perfectly what he is
doing. The coolness of Mr. Gosse's judgment is
reflected in the quality of his prose. It is quiet, even,
very compact, full of brief felicities of phrase, and
it has an agreeable tinge of acidity. He says in his
paper on Lady Ritchie that " the dish of banana
fritters is delicious, but too sweet ; a dash of lemon
would vastly improve it." His own banana fritters
never lack the dash, but they are never drowned
with the flavouring. No one could convey condemnation or ridicule in fewer or more temperate words ;
he can knock a man down with a debonair touch.
" It is," he says of one book, " felicitous in expression, and chivalrous in sentiment, but it does not
make any strong impact on the attention." Here, as
in the confection of certain cordials, the sugar has
been merely rubbed against the outside skin of the
lemon. How agreeably he says that " Villon was a

very great poet ; he was also a rogue and a robber, who committed murder too often for the occurrence to be an accident," and that " In 1861 Clough read ' Mari Magno ' to Tennyson, and cried like a child over it. We are not told whether Tennyson wept," and that " People who argue that Shakespeare cannot have existed because we know so little about his life, will be pained to observe that we know still less about Massinger's." Of M. Claudel, he remarks that " His new piece is entitled ' Le Père Humilié,' but if I am asked why, it is I who am humiliated, for I have not the least idea," and of a venerable but archaistic English writer that " Mr. Doughty is very fond of ' derne ' ; his pilgrims are all suddenly dasht on a derne cliff. It sounds like a mild American expletive." Every essay he writes is sprinkled with comments like these, which produce in the reader a silent grin of enjoyment. He scorns phrase-making, but there is no living writer whose phrases are more adequate or more flavoured with personality. And this extends to his imagery. Whatever the tenour of his argument, he is liable to drop into an easy and compact metaphor, grotesque or charming, with the right imaginative touch. He speaks of two forgotten novels as " those faded romances whose very names now sound dim and faint, like the tunes of a hurdy-gurdy heard in the evening three streets off." Of the romantic generation of critics he says that " Those who marched with flags to fling themselves at the feet of Webster merely touched their sombreros lightly as they hurried past the figure of Massinger," and he sums up the whole saintly failure of Clough when he remarks that " he sat counting the pulse of his own conscience until he heard no other sound." And how better could he have conveyed the strange thrills which the biblipohile would feel in the presence of certain rare pamphlets than by this brief comparison : " Anyone casually lighting upon any of these will be like a sportsman who penetrates the brushwood of New Zealand and stalks a living moa."

These essays are delightful for their information, for their criticisms, for the biographical and auto-biographical peeps into the past which Mr. Gosse so often allows himself, and, as I have said, for the charm and pungency of their detail. But their merits of style go beyond their separate sentences. They generally have form, a considered outline, effective beginnings and effective endings. And at intervals Mr. Gosse rises into sustained eloquence. Eloquence is not his *métier*. It pertains chiefly to the enthusiast, the man who surrenders himself, and however Mr. Beerbohm may see fit to delineate Mr. Gosse he will never draw him, I think, with whirling arms, shouting himself red in the face. The style is the man, and Mr. Gosse's style is normally crisp. But his sentences join ; he has his swifter moments even if he does elevate restraint into a high place among the literary and other virtues. I do not see how I could better illustrate what he can do at times with the paragraph than by quoting his last words, quick in movement though packed with the results of reflection, on Donne :

The world, therefore, is to be excused if, while clasping Donne to its heart as a poet, it has been content to take him for granted as a prose-writer. He wrote most detestable prose in an age which had not yet strained the language of common life through the jelly-bag. All the torrent which poured from his lips as he stood, a monument of awful death in life, in his pulpit in the old Gothic Cathedral of St. Paul's was turbid with the refuse of scholastic Latin, and stained with the experiments of an English still unrefined. After all, when people like Taine speak of the great English divines as a sort of ichthyosaurians wallowing in the slime of their own obscure diction, we may recall that the mundane and playful writers of that age, like Dekker and Rowlands, are not more limpid nor much easier to read than the theologians. The fact is that, with a few bright exceptions, prose did not exist in any real lucidity and grace until the middle of the century, and English style had no Calvin to clarify its cloudiness till Jeremy Taylor rose in all his splendour. Donne is perhaps worse than the rest in certain qualities and relations, but he is better than almost all at certain moments of inspiration and glory.

It is already some time since Mr. Gosse celebrated his seventieth birthday. This book is a proof not merely of an uncanny and almost unexampled power in him of preserving his youth, and, often, bettering the achievements of his mature manhood, but also of his rare and whole-hearted devotion to and pride in the art of letters.

# THE ART OF WRITING

PROFESSOR BROWN teaches Rhetoric and Composition in Carleton College. His title-page informs us that he is the author of " How the French Boy Learns to Write." But the present book, *The Writer's Art*, is almost entirely the work of other authors : Hazlitt, Emerson, Stevenson, Thoreau, Diderot, Maupassant, Poe, and other artists who have discussed composition. The collection is primarily meant for " college use," and it is symptomatic of certain recent developments in the American academic world.

Instruction in the practice of composition is now commonly given in many American Universities, and there are signs of its approach here. I have heard of an American lady who took her Ph.D. in Short Story Writing. Manuals on that art abound in America. The kinds of short stories are classified, modes of progression are analysed, and lists which purport to be exhaustive of permissible " ingredients " are set down. I have not yet seen, though I am prepared to believe in their existence, handbooks on the composition of poetry, but an extensive literature is ávailable for aspiring dramatists, and works of a general character which, like the present anthology, are intended to assist the writer, in whatever kind, to know himself and perfect his expression, are numerous. In this country students of English are being more and more encouraged to " show up " original compositions, and teachers like Sir Arthur Quiller-Couch are propounding from lecture platforms those elementary principles of good writing which are commonly agreed upon by good writers conscious of the nature of their own activities.

I do not know that "Q" or his colleagues have ever supposed or suggested that their maxims would lead to an increase in the production of good literature. Their practice is defensible without resort to that contention. Nobody can deny that even economists, philosophers, civil servants, and business men would be better for the acquisition of a sound English style. Sir Arthur, following in the steps of Hazlitt, Stevenson, and the rest, demands accuracy, lucidity, the concrete word rather than the abstract, the suppression of superfluous epithets, the elimination of clichés. No contributor to a Blue Book but would be better for the adoption of these counsels. Whether the inculcation of them to the undergraduate population at large will lead to a general raising of the level of written English, remains to be discovered. It is at least conceivable that nobody really comprehends this kind of teaching except those who have no need of it. I doubt this ; I am even prepared to believe that the practice of formal composition in English may assist men to read intelligently, just as the practice of Latin verse—hallowed by long tradition—is admitted to have increased men's enjoyment of their classics. But when it comes to the view that " literary artists," as they are called, may be increased in number by University courses we are on other ground. Professor Brown disclaims the notion that the whole secret of literature can be analysed, set down, and transferred. But he is remarkably optimistic all the same. " If," he says, " we are to have groups of young writers who shall contribute anything to American letters, they must receive, in addition to basic instruction, a variety of quickening suggestion, in order that they may always be open-minded and imbued with an undying intellectual curiosity." That strange sentence is succeeded by another even stranger. It deserves the prominence of an " indent " :

Very few colleges or universities encourage teachers to improve their teaching by becoming creative writers.

There it is, baldly. The teachers are to become " creative writers "—the taught—the young writers whose technical training, he says, is so inferior to that of the young engineers—are to receive, en masse, basic instruction and quickening suggestion. They are there in crowds : student-men of letters with men like Professor Brown pouring into them all the best precepts of the best writers, examining for them the best French, English, and ancient models, pruning and clipping the first productions of their craft. Teachers and students are equally eager that the next generation of American writers should be a credit to their country. But when all this labour has been given time to produce results, when the latest race of students have gone out into the world, may a new movement be expected ? When the pie is opened will the birds really begin to sing ?

Do not expect it. Men and writers may be taught much. To take a small and obvious example, an American student might be persuaded not to use " some " as an adverb, and if he were persuaded he would have been benefited. Every man has faults of expression, habitual woolly and slipshod phrases, words which he uses in wrong senses ; much may be done in the way of purging. But the future of our literature does not repose on the efforts of professors to eliminate what our ancestors called incorrectness. An intelligent man may, as the result of instruction, become a competent tradesman in written commodities of a humble kind, though even in the lowest spheres of composition a large part must be played by incommunicable faculty. The writer of a really successful soap advertisement must have a touch of genius of a kind : imagination, psychological insight, sympathy (however tinged with cynicism) with the thoughts and emotions of multitudes of people unseen. Yet if even in the lower walks all is not done when certain minor faults have been eliminated, and a shop-finish produced, how is it when we are in the world where men write for immortality ? The most constant and awful thoughts and the deepest passions of men, the hopes they have when they are in love and their fears when they contemplate death, are the themes. A variety of characters are displayed, panoramically and in their separate reactions : or a man sets down his own heart. The truth must be seen and told, and in such actions that emotion is conveyed from writer to reader. The fundamental elements in literature are often enough insisted upon in the extracts given by Professor Brown. Not merely have the great laid emphasis upon them, but Professor Brown has found them stated in a leading article from the *New York Sun*, which I may quote because of its unexpectedness :

You don't find feelings in written words unless there were feelings in the man who used them. With all their apparent independence they seem to be little vessels that hold in some puzzling fashion exactly what he put into them. You can put tears into them as though they were so many little buckets ; and you can hang smiles along them, like Monday's clothes on the line, or you can starch them with facts and stand them up like a picket-fence ; but you won't get the tears out unless you first put them in. Art won't put them there. It is like the faculty of getting the quality of interest into pictures. If the quality exists in the artist's mind, he is likely to find means to get it into his pictures, but if it isn't in the man no technical skill will supply it.

A man may do much for another man. But, in the literary as in other worlds, it is of little real use to tell him cold-bloodedly that honesty is the best policy. A conviction that the truth ought to be told, and the expression of it striven for, is scarcely a matter to be conveyed by pedagogics ; and a thousand lectures about the artistic necessity of sincerity and humanity will not unseal the fountains of the heart. Artistic genius, though often found in immoral surroundings, has a moral quality. If a man incapable of writing literature can at all be made into a man capable of it the change will be the result of a kind of conversion. And strong moral influence is neither more nor less likely to be exercised by a teacher of literature than by a teacher of any other subject—including theology. When the American revival comes I doubt if the schools will have much to do with it.

After this digression, if it be a digression, I will return for a moment to Professor Brown's book. It is an admirable book of its kind. He has gone far afield for his extracts ; he includes, amongst other things, Edward Coplestone's delicious adverse review of Milton, and he has made his explanatory notes as short as possible. It should be useful, and it is extremely readable : an anthology of good prose which, since it was made in order to serve a special purpose, contains none of those familiar purple passages without which no ordinary collection of prose masterpieces dare show its face in public.

# A METABIOLOGICAL PENTATEUCH

IT would have been a pity not to use it at the top of the page. I remember learning, when still young enough to think long words amusing, a poem about the adventures of " an antediluvian man of sesquipedalian height " who met an ichthyosaurus. Mr. Shaw's sub-title recalls that ; but he may be allowed his little jokes. He is far too shrewd a journalist to employ these terms for his main titles. No sub-editor on an evening paper ever had a better gift for pungent and arresting headlines. " Back to Methuselah " is one of the happiest conceptions he has had ; it catches one at once, and has the added advantage of meaning something. This, however, is what the reader does not understand immediately : there is, as usual, a preface interposed between the title-page and the play.

It is a long preface and not in every respect one of Mr. Shaw's best. The History of Evolutionary Thought is surveyed, with glances at the theatre, painting, politics, and theology. Mr. Shaw races along with fewer good witticisms than usual and fewer really provocative remarks. The sensation of speed is enjoyable at first. But after a while one tends to drowse ; one ceases to notice the swift succession of passing objects, and is conscious only of the rhythmic rattle of the train. The upshot of it is that Creative Evolution is " the genuinely scientific religion for which all wise men are now anxiously looking." Our old friend, the Life Force, comes in (he always reminds me, by the way, of Gibbon's sneer about " the science, or rather the language of metaphysics ") as the motive power. The play that follows has a major and a minor theme. The major is Creative Evolution at work—mind conquering matter. The minor is a new instrument for accelerating the process. Men do not live long enough to learn anything. They are children—none more so than Mr. Asquith and Mr. Lloyd George. Lamarck teaches that if a species wants anything badly it will get it. Men should want to live to the age of Methuselah, instead of dying in their intellectual infancy. If they did the evolutionary movement would proceed much more quickly and win far more commendation than it does from Mr. Shaw.

Certain stages of it are presented in Mr. Shaw's five Acts. He begins with an allegorical picture of Adam and Eve in the garden, and the suggestions of the snake, whence came Death and all our Woe. We next come to the present day, when the theory of volitional survival is formulated to a pair of stupid and incredulous politicians, a curate and a hoyden with bobbed hair. Next, in 2170, we find a man actually surviving for three hundred years (persons of normal age, in spite of mechanical advance, remaining as foolish and greedy as ever), and finally we come to A.D. 31920. That is not Utopia ; Mr. Shaw's only Perfect State is the Eternity of the Spirit. But people are now born from eggs, in a condition corresponding to our condition at seventeen ; they outgrow mundane passions and affections in four years ; and the more elderly are safely and consciously forwarding a further movement away from our present plight. Lilith, the *dea ex machina*, at the close proclaims the aim : " I shall see the slave set free and the enemy reconciled, the whirlpool become all life and no matter."

The drama itself occupies 267 pages. At the close of the preface Mr. Shaw says : " I am doing the best I can at my age. My powers are waning ; but so much the better for those who found me unbearably brilliant when I was in my prime." The admission is so handsome and so unusual that it seems almost a pity that it was unnecessary. Mr. Shaw's powers do not seem to be waning at all. The only typically senile vice that he has is the vice of garrulity, and that in him, to use the jargon which so delights him, was rather an inherited predisposition than an acquired habit. His juniors would be perfectly prepared to believe that, like the people in his last act, he was born from an egg and began discoursing when no more than his head was through the shell. But that his powers are waning there is no evidence at all in this book. Those who creep back to him in the belief that he has become completely mild and tame will be disagreeably surprised. His life differs from his play in this, that it is not merely the ghost of the Old Adam that is appearing in the last act. Mr. Shaw is as clever, as vigorous, as cunning, as high-spirited, as flippant, as curious as ever he was. There are conspicuous faults in this book. The preface, for all its merits, is rather inconsecutive, and gives one the feeling that although Mr. Shaw habitually thinks, he seldom stops to think. His characters are mostly sticks ; his appeal is almost continuously to the intellect ; the text is overloaded with topical references ; a few passages are in bad taste and many

pages are tiresome. Most of the middle of the play
might have been taken for granted ; we did not
want that endless silly talk between Mr. Lloyd
George, Mr. Asquith, and the rest, to help us form
a conception of the present limitations of humanity;
some scene much shorter could have furnished the
necessary symbol. But there is no reason to trace
any of these things to senile decay.

Mr. Shaw's qualities and faculties are precisely
what they were ; the faculty of being very boring
was always amongst them, and he may cheer himself with the reflection that there is no fault here,
large or small, which cannot be paralleled repeatedly
from his earlier plays. I at least feel that in places
Mr. Shaw is here surpassing his previous best, and
notably in the first and last scenes. The whole play
may be no more actable than the second part of
" Faust " or yesterday's *Times*, but the first act and
part of the last would be as effective in the theatre
as anything that Mr. Shaw has ever done. The
craftsmanship of the Eden scene deserves the much-
abused epithet, " astonishing " ; every sentence is
revelatory, and moves the action forward ; and the
whole is a genuine re-creation of the legend. The
illusion is perfectly imposed, and the temptation to
cheap cleverness, which previous wits who have
dealt with that story have not resisted, is avoided.
Mr. Shaw's sympathy with the Serpent is scarcely
veiled, but he does not obscure his intellectual conceptions with irrelevant jests as he has so often done,
nor does he allow those conceptions, in their turn,
to smother the dramatic progress of his story. In
the last act he comes nearer to poetry than he has

ever come, and in the last pages nearer to awe. An operation would have to be performed on him before he could actually write poetry or communicate awe ; but the operation would cut something out, not put something in. There are elements in his composition which inhibit him from an even momentary abandonment to love or pity or æsthetic enjoyment, and he is incapable of fear. He is always " all there " ; he possesses his subject and cannot be possessed by it ; his sense of humour is never in complete abeyance ; the strain of argument is always present ; he is too interested in things in general to give his natural sympathy for individuals much play—being, like Nature, careful of the race, but careless of the single specimen ; he despises the senses and, in so far as Art appeals to the senses, he despises Art. When he uses the mechanism of Strephon and Amaryllis, temple and bosky glade and pastoral dance, in the last act, our constant tendency to lapse into enjoyment of the idyllic element is checked by the pervasive sense of Mr. Shaw's irony ; we know he thinks that all nonsense. Even at the close where, as I have said, he does actually come near awe, he does not quite achieve it : for in the imagined presence of the very spirit of Nature, to whom he has dedicated himself, Mr. Shaw's self-possession and detachment remain : it is as it were a theoretical awe struggling to carry conviction. Nevertheless, that scene, from the procession of primæval ghosts to the last eloquent harangue of the symbolic Lilith, is conceived finely, and constructed with extraordinary skill. It leaves one with a sense of having had a glimpse of grandeur.

A cold and pagan grandeur ; but there is Mr. Shaw's philosophy. He is unlike Mr. Wells in many respects, but he is like him in this, that so long as he can regard himself as a humble instrument of Evolution he is perfectly happy. His horizon is wider than Mr. Wells's, and the operation of his revered process more extensive. Mr. Wells, except for an occasional dash into metaphysics just to show that he knows they are there, usually keeps his eyes firmly glued on the earth, which was once a whirling ball of fire. Time is good enough for him, and if the upward climb from the amœba is going to end in a material calamity, collision or cooling, he prefers not to worry about it. He advocates our co-operation with the biological movement as a man advocates any other measure of practical reform. Mr. Shaw is not satisfied with that. He has always been interested in the physical details of current evolutionary science. He will talk about Darwin, Lamarck, and Weismann until all's blue, and in the present preface he very nearly does. But his Adam and Eve is only a metaphysical parable. He is not content to begin with the amœba, or to end with a race of very highly educated engineers who play billiards on board their smoothly-running trains or discover how to fly to the other planets. Vegetarian, teetotaler, anti-æsthete, he does not really long to increase material comforts or delights ; he wants to abolish them and the means of enjoying them.

His final blissful dream is of man shedding one organ after another, the foot, the hand, the head, until he becomes pure spirit : Creative Evolution. I hold no brief for Mr. Asquith or Mr. Lloyd

George, but I doubt whether they would be justified in taking it from Mr. Shaw that the democracy has given them a mandate for this. No doubt they look grotesque little objects when Mr. Shaw exhibits them in front of a background of æons. But it is a tough test. Even the majestic author of this preface might appear slightly ridiculous were he conceived as delivering his soul under the shadow of something no larger or more ancient than the Pyramids and the Parthenon. Nevertheless Mr. Shaw has attempted to formulate his view of things and his ideal ; and the attempt must command respect. Even he, with all his desire, has not bridged the passage from Time to Eternity in his exposition : but the difficulty of relating two things, neither of which one can comprehend, is no new one. Mr. Shaw announces that he has done his best to provide mankind with the Bible of a new religion : a demand for which has just been made by Mr. Wells. It may be taken for certain that mankind at large, if it ever hears of them, will find his dogmas about life eternal as vague as it will find his dogmas on life temporal unappetising. Put it in another manner. Are you yourself quite happy with the notion of the Universe as an enormous theatre where one long Shaw play is being acted ? I don't think Bibles are made this way.

# BYRON

*ASTARTE* was first published in 1905. Its author, Lord Lovelace, was Byron's grandson. Its theme was the guilt of Byron and his half-sister, Mrs. Leigh. The first edition was very small. Lord Lovelace desired " above all things to avoid the possibility of making money out of the story " of his ancestors, and most of the copies were given away to his friends. Occasionally some of them have come into the salerooms and fetched as much as twenty pounds each. The contents of the book were universally known, but not generally accessible. This situation was clearly unsatisfactory, the last thing Lord Lovelace wanted being to cater for speculators in the *chronique scandaleuse*. Beyond this there was the fact that some people held he had not fully proved his case, and the family possessed documents, unpublished by him, which supplemented his evidence. His widow, therefore, has now produced a comparatively cheap and enlarged edition through the ordinary publishing channels.

What made Lord Lovelace attempt so repellent a task ? He would have been in ordinary circumstances the last man to do so ; a studious and fastidious man who disliked publicity of any kind, and whose loathing of gossip, prying journalism, and what seemed to him the thousand squalid vulgarities of modern civilisation, bordered on eccentricity. Had the charge never been made against Byron he would have been the last to break silence. But it had been made, it had been incompetently made (by Mrs. Beecher Stowe, who had, he thought, betrayed Lady Byron's confidence), it had been bitterly answered by Byron's friends, who had accused Lady Byron of coldly and cruelly ruining his life, and he felt that justice demanded that Lady Byron's memory should be cleared. He could do nothing for his grandfather's reputation, but he might at least secure that justice should be done to the innocent woman whose life his grandfather had wrecked. With great reluctance, therefore, he sorted his family papers—memoranda by Lady Byron and her friends, letters from Lady Byron, Lord Byron, and Mrs. Leigh, and others, unpublished material of every description—and made out his case, supporting his arguments with quotations from the poems.

His evidence will not be analysed here, and it may be left to those who like such things to pad their columns with the most ardent sentences, the darkest hints and the most suspicious parentheses in the letters which passed between Byron and his half-sister. The case made out is undoubtedly very strong, and probably at this date could not be answered ; but, whatever may be the temptation to take the matter as settled, it must in fairness be admitted that the last degree of proof is lacking, the few direct sentences of testimony or confession which would outweigh all the rest put together. Lady Byron's tenderness and goodness are certainly demonstrated ; it is also clear that she believed her husband guilty of the enormity ; and it always has been clear that the Byron with whom she spent her year of married life was a man who gave her plenty of reasons for leaving him, without recourse to that now under discussion. He paraded his infidelities, and his temper was so bad that close observers believed him to be deranged ; wounded pride and his great gift for self-pity accounted for the pathetic, half-genuine, later protestations that she had heartlessly deserted him ; he had taken small pains to make her happy when she was present. Even if we assume every one of Lord Lovelace's contentions to be true, they make little difference in one's conception of Byron's character. This may seem an extreme thing to say. But he had one of the most puzzling characters on record, and in his rages of pride, rebellion, and desire he was capable of anything.

His hand was against every man and every institution. He had deliberately willed not to govern his almost ungovernable passions. There were things he would have shrunk from doing. He disliked lying (there seems to have been a fear that he would even tell the truth about his relations with Mrs. Leigh, and certainly nothing but solicitude for her would have restrained him), he would never have been cruel for cruelty's sake, and he was incapable of an underhand plot against any man's life or reputation. It was not only " the pageant of his bleeding heart " that he was willing to trail across Europe : Europe could know everything about him. No doubt this scorn of concealment was not mainly meritorious ; telling the truth was one way of securing the " glory " for which he hungered, and the more shocking the truth, the greater the glory. A more lunatic pride than his has never been known, and it was from that that his rebelliousness mainly sprang. Shelley was the rebel of love, Byron the rebel of hate and contempt. Shelley believed in a Utopia, Byron had no such illusions. He felt himself superior to the rest of mankind ; like Napoleon, he conceived that morality was not made for him ; he was Satan in revolt. The Biblical comparison is not inapt. He was soaked in Biblical phraseology and might have used it himself ; but beyond that there was a strain of belief in him. A common egoist and roué does not habitually employ terms like " sin," " guilt," and " crime," which constantly haunted Byron's mind and verses.

Byron was a paradox even more than other men are. He had a conscience which never modified his conduct, a refinement which could not mitigate his coarseness, a kindness which was obscured at the smallest firing of his pride or his desire, and, oddest of all, a sense of humour which never assisted him to observe proportion. " Heaven knows why," wrote the exile from Geneva, " but I seem destined to set people by the ears." If this were serious it would be staggering ; if it be facetious it is most difficult to reconcile conduct which was frequently not that merely of a reckless and cheerful libertine, but that of a savage, tigerish, mad. All the indictments of him ever written fade from memory as one reads the sunny cynicism of his letters and " Don Juan," as they do when one comes across his gentler lyrics or remembers the many stories of his generosity and good companionship. He was capable, sometimes, even of humility ; he said that if people only knew Shelley's writings they would realise how second-rate were his own. According as people like his poetry or not, or according as temperament or caprice lead them to fasten upon one or another aspect of his career and character, so they are " pro " or " con." Nobody has yet succeeded (and few have seriously attempted it) in reconciling all his aspects. Any full description must always look like a tessellated pavement, with alternate squares of black and white.

A thousand new books will fail to solve the riddle, and a thousand new crimes would not entirely destroy the affection that many people must feel for him. Those who were disgusted by his anger and his sneers were fascinated again by his smile ; those who knew that he exploited his charm could not deny his charm ; and it is in death as it was in life. As for his poetry, concerning which it is time that somebody said something, it may seldom be the best kind of poetry, but much of it is living literature. Except in some of the narratives, where unconvincing stories were rhetorically told in language that seldom passed eloquence, he always worked on the true materials of poetry. His sufferings, however self-induced, were real, and he had a genuine, if not a real passion for Nature ; he watched the general spectacle of the human world with immense gusto, and he was moved to awe by the fundamental problems of existence. As a writer of satirical verse it may be maintained (though he himself would have regarded this as blasphemy against Pope) that he is unequalled, if combined quality and quantity be considered, in our language. The satirist in him—the same thing happened in Pope—

tended, as time went on, to overmaster the rest. The faults of his serious poetry are partly faults of exaggeration, natural to a glutton for personal fame who was desirous of impressing the grandeur of his moods upon mankind, and partly faults of expression. He had, although an immense gift for compact, neat, and antithetical lines, a defective ear. His dislike of the looser measures which had superseded the couplet went with an incapacity to use them with very much finesse. And he did not care about fine shades of phrasing ; the first vigorous words which came to his pen would do. So immense a production, considering his various occupations, could scarcely have been managed otherwise. The consequence has been a reaction which has accused him of writing fustian, false rhetoric, and jingling prose. But even at his worst it is difficult to stop reading him, for the quickened pulse is behind what he writes, and, with whatever lack of care, he did frequently in his heat express genuine sentiments with consummate naturalness. Passages simple, sincere, moving, reflecting the elementary impulses of the human breast, may be found throughout his works, from the early affecting poems addressed to his Harrow friends to the last lines he wrote at Missolonghi :

> Seek out—less often sought than found—
> A soldier's grave, for thee the best ;
> Then look around, and choose thy ground
> And take thy rest.

Whatever he had done he had not been happy. The lightning he had defied had struck him. His desire for peace was genuine, and at the end he was familiar with the most pitiful and awful mood a man can have—the mood in which he does not care whether he lives or dies. At the end he died in a good cause, and whatever may be disclosed about him his statues will stand about the towns of Greece. What drove him there ? Not an abstract passion for liberty, but a romantic attachment to historic Greece and his European, his almost John Bullish, instincts, which roused him to resist the Orient which so fascinated him. He had written about Marathon ; he never lived to hear of Mustapha Kemal. Unconsciously he was a prominent figure in a struggle which has gone on for thousands of years, the struggle between East and West over the body and soul of the Levant. He lived a scoffer and died a Crusader, and there are some graves over which it becomes us to show a little charity, though we mustn't, more than we can help, lie.

I have got away from " Astarte." It is a work of great labour, conceived and executed conscientiously. But it is rather a document put in as evidence than a book which can be recommended to those who wish to be edified or amused.

# MR. DE LA MARE'S ROMANCE

FIVE years ago it might still have been desirable, when nominally reviewing a book of prose by Mr. de la Mare, to occupy oneself entirely with proclaiming the merits of his verse. This is not necessary to-day. He stole very slowly and unobtrusively into public notice, producing little, never adapting himself to an assumed public taste, oblivious to every kind of advertisement, content to express what was true to him and resolved to employ every resource of his art on every line of his work. But there is now no lover of poetry willing to dispute his place among the immortals ; the certainty of his progress has equalled its tranquillity ; he is admitted to be as true a poet and as consummate an artist as any man who ever wrote English lyrics. His prose, of which there are several long examples, is not so widely known or appreciated as " Motley " and " Peacock Pie." Those who think that a poet is wasting his time if he takes serious pains with anything but poetry will think this fitting. But after reading " Memoirs of a Midget " it is impossible to be wholehearted in one's regret that he should have devoted years of labour to so full and beautiful a work.

A sketch of the plot of this romance will give a very poor notion of its nature. Miss M., the Midget, is exceedingly small, smaller than the common dwarf, almost elfin in size. She passes in succession through home life, life in a small town, life in fashionable London, then has a brief turn in a circus, and retires into country peace. Well, we can conceive novels about dwarfs: Dickens might have written one, and very comic and pathetic it would have been. But Mr. de la Mare's book is profoundly unlike a novel by Dickens or anybody else. There is a story. There are episodes, such as that of proud, heartless, beautiful Fanny and the curate, which might have been conceived by another. But the library subscriber who should carry the book off under the impression that she was taking an ordinary narrative fiction home would have a shock. For, good as are many of the characters and the events that happen to them, they are seen through a lens of whimsicality. And the main quality of the book is not that it enlists our sympathies for particular men and women, or gives us a realistic presentation of scenes from the human comedy as we know it, but that it introduces us into Mr. de la Mare's world, and brings us into contact with his feelings about the life which detached Miss M. saw us leading with such pathetic courage and blindness. It is a poet's book. I can think of no prose book by an English poet which is a more substantial achievement, but of many in which poets have escaped to a greater extent from the manner and matter of their poetry. Mr. de la Mare is one and indivisible. The world of his poetry, that strange assembly of pictures and sentiments drawn in from the daily world, from childhood's memories, and from art, contains elements familiar separately but nowhere else found in such combination. He can write of familiar decorative things, a deserted garden, or a statue in a fountain, as though nobody had ever seen them before : he makes everything he touches his, and he touches nothing to which he does not sincerely respond. The world of his poetry is a quiet world of moonlight in still places, of evening waters, of gardens, woods, and wild roses, of quiet parlours sleeping in sunlight, of midnight silences broken by small sounds. Yet it is a world never made for decoration ; it is haunted by the most secret whispers of the heart, and in every corner of it we encounter a gentle, bewildered, suffering human spirit. In a lyric the quintessence of a chapter can be given, and made memorable by music. The music, largely, has gone from Mr. de la Mare's prose ; but in this romance it is his old world we see again and in immensely greater detail.

The book is a close tissue of lovely images and perfect phrases. Every page is crowded, so crowded that it can be read only slowly if the mind's eye will see everything that is presented to it and the heart receive every quiet message. But in all this elaboration and complication of picture and language, thought, and fancy, there is never anything false or faked, not a word that is dishonest, or that strikes one as having been put in for effect. The major elements in our landscape are shown with surpassing freshness : the Midget helps here, for she was secluded until grown up, and the author, looking through her unaccustomed eyes, has realised many common things—the stars over a wood, the sensation of being alone in the fields at night, the sea, trains, tea-parties, streets—as though they had all just broken on him for the first time. There are countless little landscapes, and the stars, with their noble names, Sirius and Aquila and Aldebaran, come in as a recurring motive, pure, keen, and remote in the night. In every chapter there are, as there were sure to be, vivid interiors : furniture shining, old women fussing, kettles boiling, cats purring, candles reflected in mirrors, moonlight ghostly through curtains, and stairs creaking in the darkness. But the most remarkable thing is the multitude of small things seen and described with loving precision. In one of the finest of his poems Mr. de la Mare has mused on the endless wonders of creation, Leviathan and the honey fly, the smooth-plumed bird :

> The seed of the grass,
> The speck of stone
> Which the way-faring ant
> Stirs—and hastes on !

The illusion of size has never blinded him ; the small things are much the more numerous and the more neglected ; he has watched them and thought on the life within them. His leviathans are few compared with his mice and snails and spiders, in a teeming world where every stone hides a community and every blossom has its secret and peculiar hieroglyphics. Miss M. in her latter retirement spent her time, we are told, " embroidering her brilliant tiny flowers and beetles and butterflies with her tiny needle." Small things had been more clear to her than to us, and many of her principal experiences had come to her through them. Cruelty, death, and decay broke upon her with the manifest destinies of mole and wren ; and her first night of fear reached its culmination with a swarm of cockroaches, " shelled, nocturnal, sour-smelling creatures . . . scurrying away into hiding, infants seemingly to their mothers, whisper, whisper." But it is Mr. de la Mare's autobiography as well as hers that we are reading when we get such confessions as this :

> Over such small things as a nut, a shell, a drop of rain-water in a buttercup, a pond of frost (for there were cold winters at Lyndsey in those days), I would pore and pore, imbibing the lesson that the eye alone, if used in patience, will tell its owner far more about an object than it can merely see.

So, when he paints the sky in all its transformations, woods and houses in all their moods, the larger outlines always contain minute details clearly seen. There are thousands of phrases which might be quoted : " Raying lights circled across the ceiling, as carriage and cart glided by on the esplanade " ; " a dwindling meteor silvered across space " ; " the forsaken sweet of the morning " . . . fruits of an eye that never fails to notice and a memory that always records. But both Mr. de la Mare's observation and the qualities of his prose may perhaps more easily be illustrated from one of the few sustained passages allowed himself by an author who writes beautifully because he writes exactly and affectionately, but never aims at the grandiose set piece or pads a paragraph to make it the length of the most approved fine paragraphs. This comes from the account of Miss M.'s childhood when she is under the roof of her father and mother and beginning to learn her universe :

> My eyes dazzled in colours. The smallest of the marvels of flowers and flies and beetles and pebbles, and the radiance that washed over them, would fill me with a mute, pent-up rapture almost unendurable. Butterflies would settle quietly on the hot stones beside me, as if to match their raiment against mine. If I proffered my hand, with quivering wings and horns they would uncoil their delicate tongues and quaff from it drops of dew or water. A solemn grasshopper would occasionally straddle across my palm, and with patience I made quite an old friend of a harvest mouse. They weigh only two to the halfpenny. This sharp-nosed furry morsel would creep swiftly along to share my crumbs and snuggle itself to sleep in my lap. By-and-by, I suppose, it took to itself a wife ; I saw it no more. Bees would rest there, the panniers of their thighs laden with pollen ; and now and then a wasp, his jaws full of wood or meat. When sun-beetles or ants drew near they would seem to pause at my whisper, as if hearkening, as if in their remote silence pondering and sharing the world with me. All childish fancy, no doubt ; for I proved far less successful with the humans.

But now that I have pulled it from the mould, I feel that it somewhat wilts and fades. It is a delicate book, not easily to be handled by coarse fingers, not even as I have said, easily to be described. There is a

wiser and sweeter son of Poe in it, and a gentler
brother of the Brontës, and a cousin of Hans
Andersen : even those traffic in the elusive, and
most of what is here can be indicated by no name
except that of de la Mare, a sufficient label for those
who know him, and nothing in the world for those
who do not. He quotes—he probably doesn't know
how often he has quoted—the old verses of " Tom
o' Bedlam," whose mistress was the moon :

> With a heart of furious fancies,
> Whereof I am commander ;
>> With a burning spear,
>> And a horse of air,
> To the wilderness I wander.

> With a knight of ghosts and shadows,
> I summoned am to tourney ;
>> Ten leagues beyond
>> The wide world's end ;
> Methinks it is no journey.

It is no more easy to catalogue Mr. de la Mare than
it is to analyse that. He has rich gifts of fancy, and
even of demure wit : many others have had as much.
He tells fairy-tales, but how far he is from being a
luxurious or sentimental dreamer ! He plays with
toys, but conscious of impending calamity ; he takes
in impressions through every sense, but how little
is he a slave of the senses ! The most dominant thing
about him is a thing, never paraded but always present : his sense of the mystery, beyond all the superficial beauty and dreadfulness, of existence :

# MR. DE LA MARE'S ROMANCE

When Music sounds all that I was I am
Ere to this haunt of brooding dust I came.

Everything, from the stars to the minutest plants, he sees against that background of eternity. If he dogmatised about it he would be more easy to talk about ; but the one thing he scarcely ever expresses is an opinion. In the recesses of his mind he has his prepossessions ; though he continually asks questions he never has the colour of a sceptic, but all his opinions are unformulated. One can say no more than that he feels the unseen behind the seen, and is awed and vaguely comforted in its presence.

Miss M., too, bravely battled under that arch, and was happy. Her story adds immensely to one's knowledge of and admiration for her creator. I cannot, however, deceive myself into thinking that it will be understood, or even read, by a large public. A few people will read it ; but those who read it at all will read it many times. It is a book for poets and their kindred, and unlike any other book that ever was written. The symbol may be queer. But are we not all Midgets, making terms with a foreign world, and tiny under the heavens ?

# CROCE ON SHAKESPEARE

BENEDETTO CROCE, the most stimulating of contemporary philosophers, has a universality of interest rare amongst modern thinkers. He proceeds with ease from pure metaphysics, ethics, and æsthetics to the consideration of the concrete results of history and the concrete achievements of art ; and the range of his knowledge is so great that he can meet the experts with equal knowledge in any field which he cares to enter. The nearest parallel we have had to him in England is Coleridge : I do not suggest that his ideas resemble Coleridge's, but Coleridge will serve as an indication of the width of his outlook, his equal gaze over the eternal and the temporal, the humanity of his philosophic writings, and the philosophic quality of his critical work.

Until this book on Shakespeare appeared—translated, rather carelessly, I am sorry to say, by his regular English interpreter, Mr. Ainslie—none of the great Italian's literary criticisms had seen the light in English. The volume is a collection of essays on three great figures—Ariosto, Corneille, and Shakespeare. If I say nothing about the papers on Ariosto and Corneille it is not only that I do not feel qualified to discuss writers with whom I have a very slight acquaintance, but that Croce himself would not pretend that those poets were on the same plane as Shakespeare or that his essays on them were of equal importance with his criticisms of Shakespeare.

His criticisms of Shakespeare, I say. But a large part of his Shakespearean treatises is devoted to criticisms of Shakespeare's critics. Signor Croce is that unusual thing, a philosopher who loves poetry for its own sake, and a critic who realises that art is something other than a vehicle for deliberate teaching. He is also a man of strong common sense and with a marked proclivity for stating facts as he sees them. The result is that the thousand and one biographers of and commentators on Shakespeare come off very badly at his hands. He writes much valuable and beautiful criticism ; his sense of poetic values is very acute ; his descriptions of such characters as Hotspur, Falstaff, and Cordelia could scarcely be bettered for eloquence and fairness. But he is largely controversial ; and his arguments are chiefly directed against those who will insist on mixing up Shakespeare's plays with Shakespeare's supposed life and opinions.

Signor Croce is penetrating and satisfying as an interpreter of Shakespeare's characters and as a delineator of his art. But in spite of all his protests he naturally goes farther than this. He attempts to discover the chief intellectual interests and spiritual predilections of Shakespeare the poet, and he also is led to implications about Shakespeare the man. He marches under no political or religious banner ; he is not the poet of particular practical ideals, *non est de hoc mundo*, because he always goes beyond, to the universal man, to the conscious problem. Signor Croce, having said this, feels obliged to gloss over the motives behind the historical plays. He is right in thumping the commentators who have attempted to deduce some modern brand of Liberalism or Toryism from the historical plays. But he is, I think,

understating the fact when he says that all that the
historical plays prove is that Shakespeare had a
keen interest in " practical action," and that " this
interest, finding its most suitable material in political
and warlike conflicts, was naturally attracted to
history, and to that especial form of it which was
nearest to the soul and to the culture of the poet of
his people and of his time, English and Roman history. This material had already been brought to the
theatre by other writers and was in this way introduced to the attention and used by the new poet."
It might certainly be put more bluntly. There is no
justification, in this instance, for divorcing the im-
aginations of the poet from the affections of the
man ; and if there is one thing clear about Shakespeare it is that he felt a peculiar affection for his
own country and that (since he was far too intelligent
not to have put the question to himself) he was
prepared to defend his patriotism on practical
grounds. There comes a point later at which Signor
Croce uses language which cannot but apply to
Shakespeare the man and arouse curiosity about
Shakespeare the citizen. He refuses to contemplate
the possibility of knowing Shakespeare's intentions
regarding Shylock, " because Shylock lives and
speaks, himself explaining what he means, without
the aid of commentaries, even such as the author
might possibly have supplied "—as though characters dropped from off Shakespeare as apples fall
from an undeliberate and unreflecting tree. But he
is firm enough about certain other of the plays. He
says of " King Lear " : " An infinite hatred for
deceitful wickedness has inspired this work " ; but

also the inspiration of love, love of goodness manifested in Cordelia, " a true and complete goodness,
not simply softness, mildness and indulgence :

Why ? Why does not goodness triumph in the
material world ? And why, thus conquered, does
she increase in beauty, evoke ever more discon-
solate desire, until she is finally adored as something sacred ? The tragedy of King Lear is penetrated throughout with this unexpressed yet
anguished interrogation, so full of the sense of the
misery of life.

The statement is unexceptionable. One cannot
question either the description of the central point
of Othello as being " the work of Iago, of that demi-
devil, of whom one might ask in vain why he had
thus noosed the bodies and souls of those men, who
had never nourished any suspicion of him ? " It is
true : he was contemplating " that most mysterious
form of evil . . . perversity, which is an end and a
joy to itself." It is equally true that

It would be vain to seek among the songs of
Shakespeare for the song of reconciliation of
quarrels, composed of inner peace, of tranquillity
achieved, but the song of justice echoes everywhere in his works.

But if it be true that Shakespeare the dramatist
meditated much on evil and good, that he had a
passion for justice, a hatred of cruelty and unkind-
ness and malice, a love of goodness and charity, is

it possible to argue that this gives us no clue to the nature of Shakespeare the man ?

We none of us, alas, live up to the best of our dreams. We may be models of good will towards mankind when sitting in our studies, removed from the world of conflicts and ambitions and temperamental incompatibilities, but we are all apt to stumble when we come down into the road. Nevertheless (and Croce would be the first to admit that Shakespeare was not a superman) it is not in nature for the personality of a good artist to be other than the personality which governs his deeds in the practical world. Shakespeare of Stratford (or, if you like, Lord Rutland, Lord Derby, Lord Oxford, or whatever other peer you fancy) may not always have been just, pure and kind ; but it is inconceivable that he cannot have constantly wished to be, or that his mind can have been otherwise than continually exercised with the problems of his own conduct. Signor Croce may be sympathised with in his reaction against the pedants who manufacture colossal supposititious lives of Shakespeare, with about ten small facts in them, and those other crass pedants who will be tracing in every incident of his plays the exact reflection of some event in his own life or some episode in the history which was being made around him. But he himself, however reluctantly, does form a picture of Shakespeare's character, of the character of a man who had to face, fight or make terms with the things which we all of us have to encounter. And why, since the character is a great, noble, and fascinating one, should we be precluded from taking an interest in it ?

# CROCE ON SHAKESPEARE

We are allowed to take an interest in the worldly fortunes of Henry V, who never existed, in the spiritual struggles of Macbeth and Hamlet, who never existed, in the happy and unhappy loves of Desdemona, Rosalind, and Romeo, who never existed ; why should it be mean and gross in us to feel a curiosity about the emotions and experiences of Shakespeare, who did exist and who, the father of them all, united the capacities and the sensibilities of all of them ? I do not go so far as the late Arthur Bullen, who (and he was one of those rare scholars whose love of poetry and taste in it could not be disputed) stated, when still young, that any serious student would be willing to give an arm and a leg in exchange for a single new fact about Shakespeare. If that be the qualification for serious studentship, I must frankly confess that until I am old and bed-ridden I shall be a non-starter ; and so, I fancy, would Shakespeare have been. But I do admit to a vast curiosity about the course and the results of Shakespeare's contact with the daily world, and not all Signor Croce's lofty rebukes will make me ashamed of it.

Consequently I am able (I take myself as the representative of a common type) to view with toleration and affection the gentlemen who spend years grubbing in the Record Office and in the obscurer corners of Elizabethan literature for new " facts " about the man who wrote the plays and the sonnets. No "fact" would change my conception of his character or modify belief in the general integrity of his life, the gentle considerateness with which he treated people, the efforts after justice

that he made in his dealings, and the purity and
generosity of his loves. A fact apparently irreconcil-
able with this conception I should treat as a fact
imperfectly known ; a fact in conformity would
give me great pleasure ; a fact which was " a simple
primrose " I should be glad of as such. And though
nothing would persuade me to spend my short life
doing this sort of research I cannot but be grateful
to those who, finding nothing better to do, consent
to be our helots and hodmen, zealously embracing
a voluntary servitude. Even the merely useful have
their place in the scheme of things. We may fully
accept Signor Croce's reservations about most of
the modern Shakespearean scholars and most of
the older ones except " Herder, Goethe, Schlegel,
Coleridge, and Manzoni." But if the work of literary
history had been left entirely to philosophers and
to men with a perfect understanding of the pro-
cesses of poetic creation and a perfect discrimination
amongst its results, very little literary history would
have been written.

This reservation made, one may certainly commend the book to everybody who takes an interest
in Shakespeare or in the poetic art. Or, one may
add, in the intellectual and moral health of our own
time. For Croce, although he has his shibboleths
like all philosophers, even if he couch them in less
obscure language than most, is at once a man in
love with life and a bracing moralist. He summarises
the last age in one sentence, roughly, if only roughly,
just. How, he asks, could Shakespeare be rightly
appreciated in an age when " the consciousness of
the distinction between liberty and passion, good

and evil, nobility and vileness, fineness and sensuality, between the lofty and the base in man, became obscured ; everything was conceived as differing in quantity, but identical in substance, and was placed in a deterministic relation with the external world."

# THE POETS AND CHILDHOOD

THIS book (*A Book of English Verse on Infancy and Childhood*, chosen by L. S. Wood), compiled with great pains and furnished with excellent notes, contains a selection of English poems dealing with childhood. The period of childhood is defined as extending over the first twelve years of life. The selection has been well made. Little, save a few carols, could be found in our early literature, and not much of any kind before the middle of the seventeenth century. The Elizabethans produced a few charming lullabies, and Shakespeare, as always, was searched not in vain. But five-sixths of the poems in the book are later in date than the year 1700.

Certain aspects of childhood have never disappeared from poetry. The baby in his mother's arms, a sight which it falls to most men's lot to contemplate with an emotion as deep as any, is an obviously universal theme. And the ancients, like ourselves, felt upon a child's death a sorrow of especial poignancy, and saw in it an emblem of many of the elementary facts of our lives, posing most powerfully the riddle of existence, and evoking most pathetically all the associations of transience and grief. Hope unfulfilled, growth cut short, beauty blasted, innocence cruelly ill-treated ; all these must lie in the death of a child, which has besides the common attributes of all deaths—the pain, the bewilderment, and the separation. Many of the most exquisite poems in this collection (which strangely does not contain the best of all, the Poet Laureate's " On a Dead Child ") have that subject.

# THE POETS AND CHILDHOOD

One of the best is a poem which the compiler strangely attributes to the seventeenth century, but which cannot conceivably have been written in the seventeenth century. It begins :

He did but float a little way
  Adown the stream of time ;
With dreamy eyes watching the ripples play,
  Or listening to their chime.
    His slender sail
    Scarce felt the gale ;
He did but float a little way,
  And, putting to the shore,
While yet it was early day,
Went calmly on his way,
  To dwell with us no more.

Yet if this be not of the seventeenth century, there are the lovely little elegies by Carew, Herrick, Ben Jonson, and Sir John Beaumont. What is not conspicuous in these poets or in anyone before Vaughan, is an avowed resort to early memories for subjects, and the mood in which modern poetry about children has mainly been written.

The change is well known, and, in any event, obvious. A tinge of the modern comes into Shakespeare's passage :

We were
Two lads that thought there was no more behind,
But such a day to-morrow as to-day,
And to be boy eternal . . . what we chang'd
Was innocence for innocence ; we knew not
The doctrine of ill-doing, nor dream'd
That any did.

153

This might well be Wordsworth, but it is unusual even for Shakespeare, in Shakespeare's age. A man's own childhood and childhood in general were subjects ignored.

What has produced the change of outlook, or at least of literary practice, is not easy to say. I have heard it urged that there is a connection between the modern hankering after childhood and the modern decay of religious belief ; that we must have an earthly Paradise behind us because we are uncertain of a Heavenly Paradise ahead of us ; but it is in the religious poets that the new interest and the new note may first be observed, and in them for the last two hundred years the tendency to dwell upon childhood, and with reverence, has almost always been present. It is common to almost all modern imaginative writers, and especially to poets. Since Vaughan and Traherne, Blake and Wordsworth, we must have learned to receive as a principal subject for poetry childhood considered particularly as a miraculous thing we have lost, and as a condition in a way spiritually superior. The compiler of this anthology seems to have been somewhat governed by this conception, and one feels that her choice has been rather restricted by a felt obligation to preserve the tone of awe.

Mr. Belloc's lines urging a child not to tear a book come not only as a relief, but as a reminder. We grown-up persons are only doing justice to ourselves in realising that not all children are impeccable in their conduct all the time. Vice is not purely the product of age, not do defects of character never come to light before the twelfth year.

# THE POETS AND CHILDHOOD

Let us recall our own childhood. Looked at from the outside—there is nothing more affecting than an early photograph of oneself—it may arouse feelings of envy and compassion. We see ourselves, under the spell of literature and in the light of the most vivid and dearest of our recollections, wandering in a timeless garden engaged in the most harmless of occupations, creatures of fairyland who barely consented to eat and drink and were as yet ignorant of the gross commerce of the world. We have a vision of childhood in the abstract, and that colours our pictures of ourselves. The child is fresh from Nature's mysterious mint, nearer, as it seems to our minds (which are enslaved by Time), to the unknown which precedes birth. Dependent on others, he has no need to engage in the coarse struggles by which we earn our bread, he has lost no illusions and become aware of no inescapable bad habits ; many temptations have never yet come his way ; and some of the more dangerous passions have not yet developed in him. It is no wonder that we use childhood in general as the image of a lost Eden, and that each individual of us has a tendency to place his own Golden Age in the past. We have lost things we shall never find again, and found things which we shall never be able to lose. All our virtues we impute to our childhood and all our vices to our maturer days ; we scarcely remember—or, if we do, we regard them as things for which nobody was responsible—the misdemeanours of our early youth ; and every word and deed which we really regret stands as a tarnish upon our manhood. But we ought not to deceive ourselves. If our early

memories are honestly searched we shall find in
them elements which hardly consort with the notion
of juvenile perfection. We were ignorant of many
things, and ignorance was mainly bliss. But the
emotional and intellectual weaknesses with which
we are now painfully familiar were there as far back
as we go, to the frontiers of babyhood, a region
from which we all emigrate with every recollection
of it blotted out. " 'Tis little joy," said Hood, " To
know I'm farther off from heaven than when I was
a boy." But on the lower shelves of memory's cata-
combs rest Falsehoods and Fears and selfish Re-
sentments, and Unhealthy Curiosities and Idle
Evasions, in form and feature much like their later
descendants. To begin to think is to begin to plot
and to deceive, to begin to feel is to begin to hate as
well as to love ; dishonesty comes with the first
games and shirking with the first duties. Children
do not commonly get drunk or wage war or establish
fraudulent bucket-shops. But you do not need to
be twelve years old to lose control of yourself or to
persecute or to cheat. This, that, and the other fault
—like the innocuous snobbery in the " Young
Visiters "—may be a merely superficial attribute
shed upon one by one's surroundings. But the
demands and the devices of the insistent ego are
there from the start. Knowledge may offer them
useful instruments, education and experience may
curb their violence. Children no less than men are
in their manner " fit for stratagems and spoils,"
and degeneracy as the years pass is not the inevitable
and invariable process. The " Darling of a pigmy
size " in this anthology seldom does anything more

forcible than halloo to get an echo ; if we cannot recall our own youth we may at least observe the children around us to see that the shades of the prison-house close around at a very early date. We all know people who have considerably improved since they were children ; who are less cruel, less wilful, more honest, more amiable, and so forth.

Yet it is not simply a false sentimentality that has made those who have written of their childhood and of the childhood of others present an idealised picture. The poets have not been merely deceived by the fresh bloom of a cheek into deducing a character more angelic than exists ; and they are not only influenced by envy of a state, in which one is protected against a harsh world, in which every want is supplied and every sorrow soothed. We have lost something; it is not so much innocence of mind or heart as freshness of imagination. Nothing is ever so beautiful as the things which were beautiful when we were small. We had newly come upon the world. Every object interested us and left a deep impression upon our minds. Every day new objects now grown common to us dawned upon our consciousness ; the edge of our enjoyment of the visible had not been dulled by usage, and there was no whispering crowd of solicitudes to interrupt the bright continuity of our day dreams. The bluest skies and the most silvery stars we know were seen by us not this year, but many years ago ; brooks and shrubs and insects, we saw them all magnified and in isolation ; every sense was its language. That keenness of observation, that freedom of imaginative adventure, as well as that leisure, a grown meditative man must envy, and no man more than a poet. The complementary truth is that most poets deliberately draw very largely upon their memories of childhood for the material of their verse. Earth, at any rate, lies about us in our infancy ; in our later years it is only very seldom that we really look to see if it is still there. The brain is preoccupied, and horn has come over the eyes. Eagerness has gone out of us, and when we look at a child the thought, clearly or dimly, is present in our minds : " You do not know what you have or what is in store for you. But I was once what you are now and you will be what I am now." The matter of morality is not, I think, necessarily involved.

# THE CLASSICS IN TRANSLATION

HERE are six more volumes of the Loeb Library, which now contains well over a hundred. The library, one of the greatest publishing schemes on record, was made possible by the enthusiasm, energy, and riches of Mr. J. Loeb, and its success must have rewarded him. In time the whole of the surviving works of Greek and Latin literature which are of the least interest to us will be available to us here, with the text on one page and a translation (usually good and sometimes brilliant) on the opposite page. The variety of the works published and the status of the translators may be gathered by a glance at the list. The contents of the new batch range from the best existing version of Herodotus to a translation of Quintilian's treatise on oratory, and a version with a vast commentary on Apollodorus's collection of Greek myths by Sir James Frazer—a work which might be regarded as a supplement to the " Golden Bough " series.

The Classics can never regain their old supremacy in our education and, consequently, will never again be so familiar an element in social intercourse as they were. We even find it hard to realise how great their influence once was. When the Grammar Schools were founded, " grammar " meant Latin grammar ; and the circumstances of the time justified the insistence laid upon the ancient tongues. The Renaissance Modernists could not wish to throw Latin and Greek over as relics of Mediævalism, for Greek was largely their own discovery, and through the medium of the old manuscripts and the old monuments worlds of new beauty and new knowledge had broken upon them, with an appeal to the imagination which we can hardly conceive. Exaggeration naturally followed ; a schoolboy learned nothing of English, nothing of history, nothing of contemporary languages, and it was difficult to pursue in later life the study of any science without an intimate acquaintance with Latin. In the nineteenth century we suddenly awoke to the fact that we were still living under the hardened crust of what had once been a living movement. We began shouldering through it, and we have now largely broken it up.

It is impossible that the Classics should recover their former place in education, and, indeed, certain that they will lose more ground than they yet have —ground which will, let us hope, be partly occupied by other human studies, and not entirely given over to laboratory " experiments." But there is something more than a just and natural reaction against them to be observed. We may see all around us a kind of passionate animus against them, a desire to oust them completely, even to obliterate them from the consciousness of the race. In some quarters you cannot mention Latin without inviting the answer " dead language," or Greek without being deemed one of those supposedly blind and besotted obscurantists, the supporters of compulsory Greek. I know some otherwise enlightened men whom I suspect of a secret desire to introduce Total Prohibition of the teaching of Latin or Greek, with a heavy punishment for illicit distillers and secret consumers. The

prejudice extends to the Greeks and Romans themselves : many people felt in Mr. Wells's " Outline
of History " an inclination to " larn " the Greeks
and Romans to be classics, to visit on them all the
sins of all the Dons. In the heat of our enthusiasm
for a Business Administration Mr. Asquith's defects
were ascribed to the fact that he took the Craven,
and the merits of Sir Barnaby Rudge, the eminent
entrepreneur, to the fact that he didn't. In some
quarters a knowledge of the Classics is regarded as
a handicap, almost as a disgrace, something that
emasculates or petrifies a man ; and deliberately
anti-democratic at that.

For this absurdity there are several reasons. In
the first place all reactions go too far : those who
find consolation in metaphors may comfort themselves with the reflection that the pendulum which
sagely stopped in the middle would not work the
clock. In the second place there is a certain amount
of envy. The tendency to think (or to pretend, for
one's own comfort) that what one doesn't know
isn't worth knowing is not confined to a few especially
vain persons. It is, in varying degrees, one of the
commonest foibles of the human race ; and those
who do not know the Classics are much more vocal
now than they were fifty years ago. Moreover, the
last strongholds of overdone classical teaching have
been the institutions of the rich ; Latin and Greek
have acquired a strong class flavour which tends to
exaggerate the jealousy felt against them. In the
third place their defenders, as a body, have frequently "asked for it." While one don is busily
translating Plato or Sophocles, ten others are telling

people that they cannot get the slightest inkling of Plato and Sophocles unless they read them in the original. The classical schoolmaster, looking disdainfully down from his antique keep (which once was as new as South Kensington), has often displayed a maddening contempt for every form of study not his own, and a deplorable lack of curiosity about the spiritual and physical world into which he has been born. Nothing else but Greek and Latin could exercise the intellectual faculties of youth. Men who apparently lacked the least tinge of wisdom talked of the classics as the only sources of wisdom, and men patently devoid of æsthetic sensibility argued, or rather stated, that no modern literature could hope to compete with the ancient—however long, apparently, it might continue to grow. Naturally a great many spirited people, listening to this sort of talk, feel a strong desire to cram their Hesiods down their throats. I have said " feel," I ought to have said " felt." For during recent years the classical don and the classical schoolmaster have become very subdued. Many of them have the air of unwanted orphans in a cold world, or decrepit wasps who are afraid of being smoked out of their nests. Youth is dashing away to engineering ; parents are making themselves felt ; they have no influence over the new race of politicians and publicists. The best of them are seriously concerned lest the value they know to lie in a classical education should be lost to the State, and those who most love the ancient literatures fear that in process of time Latin and Greek might really become dead languages.

Let us hope not, though we are still not in a

position to guess what proportion, even of the most studious boys, would choose Greek and Latin for subjects of study were heavy premiums not put upon those subjects. In another generation there will certainly be fewer people who can quote Horace than now, even in the House of Lords, the only place where it is still done (about once in six months) without producing a smile or a scoff. The proportion of scholarships given to the classics will certainly diminish, and they will probably have vanished as compulsory subjects from the most conservative of our schools. Yet I cannot but think that as soon as their privileges have been removed they will call with a new fascination to many young men ; that persons, even, who have had no proper groundwork at school, will, at the period of intellectual awakening, take to the Classics with something of the zest and energy with which young men now take to other fresh studies. From the general point of view— once the admission has been made that the Classics can be replaced as *necessary* elements in the training of a fully educated man—there will be no need of a very large body of competent classical scholars. The bulk of the textual work on the existing Classics has been done ; no great percentage of European classical scholars is directly engaged in digesting and elucidating the fruits, manuscript and other, of current archæological research ; and even productive digging will come to an end in time.

So far as our civilisation is concerned the essential thing is that access to the thought and records of the Greeks and Latins should be easy. And common sense insists that this access may be open through translations—which, by the way, must, as a rule, be renewed from age to age. Classical poetry in translation—save in rare fragments done by great poets and not by great scholars—naturally loses as much as English poetry would lose if translated into Latin. Prose style may often be incommunicable in translation. Yet what proportion even of reputable scholars have read the Classics primarily as an æsthetic experience ? And how tiny a fraction of those who have, in any age, gone through the classical mill have gone through life with their Homers or their Virgils in their coat pockets ! It was not Homer's " Iliad," but Pope's, that sold twenty thousand copies in the time of Queen Anne, who is dead. Even here it cannot be granted that all is lost if there be no first-hand reading : Shakespeare probably and Keats certainly are evidence to the contrary. But in a more general way it may be argued most forcibly that one who should know the corpus of the Classics, poetical, historical, philosophical, through translations might have a far profounder appreciation of the mind, morals, and arts of Athens and Rome than many of the finest scholars on record. I once heard a classical don maintain with heat that you could not discuss the ancient literatures if you knew them only in translations ("no word was ever an exact rendering of another word," etc.), and a moment after proceed to dogmatise about Tolstoi and Turgenev for all he was worth. Yet he did not know a word of Russian. Who, except Mrs. Garnett, Mr. Baring, Mr. Harold Williams, and a few others, does ?

If (which Heaven prevent) all the classical texts

were to disappear, and only the English pages of the Loeb library were to survive, we should go on discussing the qualities and achievements of the ancients, and (excepting that those who really know would not in each generation exercise their authority to keep up a reverence for the supreme expression of certain of the poets) we should not be greatly handicapped in making our estimates, in drawing suggestions from ancient thought, or warnings from ancient experience. Even to-day our classics may read Aristotle in the original, but our political scientists usually do not. If it be true that Plutarch was partly responsible for the French revolution, he would have been (probably was) just as efficacious in translation as in the original. So if we cannot restore the widespread study of the originals we may at least try to promote a knowledge of translations more general than ever before. They are even, as a rule (it may be worth suggesting), good reading. There are dull classical as there are dull modern books ; but it is a remarkably low proportion of those which have survived. I open the second volume of Mr. A. D. Godley's exquisite version of Herodotus at random, and this is what I see : " The Budini are native to the soil ; they are nomads, and the only people in these parts that eat fir-cones." I think I shall go on from there.

# ESCAPES

EVEN a convict escaped from Dartmoor commands almost universal sympathy. Provided, in his efforts to get to safety, he merely steals clothes and food and does not commit murderous assaults, the secret good wishes of the most respectable people are with him. He may be a professional blackguard, brutal, unscrupulous, and evil of countenance, but it doesn't matter. He has shown courage and cleverness ; he has pitted himself against society, this time in an enterprise which is in itself innocent ; he is a small thing hunted by a big thing ; and we all hope he will get away—provided always, be it understood, that there is no likelihood of his appearing through our own window at dead of night. The qualities of gameness and adventurousness, the Thermopylæ element in the unequal contest, appeal to human nature so strongly that for a generation the unspeakable villain Charles (affectionately Charlie, like Mr. Chaplin) Peace was almost a popular hero, whilst reprobation was reserved for the woman who was supposed to have " done him in." Nobody, whatever public approval may be expressed, really likes the person who gives information about an escaped criminal. Here, as so often, the conscientious man has to deplore a conflict between his civic sense and his natural instincts.

Every escape is interesting, and every escaped prisoner arouses our sympathy. The best of the stories of escape from Germany will be as thrilling as ever twenty years hence, when most of the histories of operations and other impersonal war books have become documents for students or less than that. The advantage is not peculiar to books about escapes. All biographical books, all stories of the personal adventures of a man or a small group have a power of holding the attention which is often lacking in works conventionally of great " importance." For one man who will read a naval history a hundred will read the life of Nelson. If Napoleon's battles are widely studied by unprofessional readers it is largely because they were fought by Napoleon. The fate of Europe hung on Marlborough's battles also, but it has always been impossible to persuade people to take an interest in them, because they neither know anything nor want to know anything about Marlborough. History is history to very few ; to most it is drama. If we are to examine great events we prefer to do it through the eyes of one man, and it is conceivable that posterity will know no more about the East African campaign than it can learn from Major Brett-Young's " Marching on Tanga," which happens to be a very personal book written in beautiful prose.

Of the good war-books of this kind perhaps the majority have been narratives of escape, and there will probably be more of them within the next few years. Those published during the war were written under a serious handicap. Nothing could be included which might assist the enemy, and no information about methods of escape which might impair the chances of anybody else escaping. There were nevertheless several which, if slight, were

extremely exciting ; amongst them Capt. Gilliland's
" My German Prisons," Captain Caunter's modest
and vivid "˛Thirteen Days," and, above all, the late
Pat O'Brien's characteristically named " Outwitting
the Hun." This author was a young American in
the British Air Force ; he was reported recently to
have been killed in an accident in a Western State.
He wrote his book slangily and with the gusto of
one who, if he had no true tall stories to tell, would
have invented false ones for the fun of telling them.
Nothing that happened to him was of an ordinary
kind. He began by nose-diving from a height of
several thousand feet and crashing without breaking a bone. He leapt off a train almost as soon as he
got into Germany. After living on roots for days he
swam the Meuse in so exhausted a condition that
he had to get rid of his wrist watch in order to re-
lieve himself of its weight. He lived in a large Belgian
town for weeks with Germans all around ; he got
into Holland by burrowing under the great German
wire-fence ; and he rounded off his exploits by
dedicating his book to the useful Pole Star, which
had probably never received such an honour before.
The book is one which may still be commended
as a true story as full of dramatic moments as
" Greenmantle " ; but the best and most elaborate
escape stories have taken longer to write and appeared later. " The Road to Endor " is now,
deservedly, in its seventh edition, and it is highly
probable that Captain Evans's book, *The Escaping
Club*, will have an equal success.

Captain Evans is the Hampshire and England
cricketer. During the Somme battle an intractable

aeroplane engine let him down in the German lines, and he spent most of the rest of the war-period escaping from captivity. He had been in Germany (the Harz district) for two months when he got well away for the first time, went by train to Dusseldorf with a Belgian confederate, spent a day there, and was ultimately caught twenty yards from the Dutch frontier. The result of this was removal to the dark, icy, insanitary, crowded Fort 9 at Ingolstadt, where were collected a large number of the toughest characters from the Allied armies. Most of them were there as punishment for escaping from other camps. They answered gross ill-treatment with perpetual insubordination, and they spent most of their time inventing and attempting every sort of ingenious scheme for getting out of an almost impossible place. In this camp there were :

Men who could make keys which would unlock any door ; men who could temper and jag the edge of an old table-knife so that it would cut iron bars ; expert photographers (very useful for copying maps) ; engineering experts who would be called in to give advice on any tunnel which was being dug ; men who spoke German perfectly ; men who shammed insanity perfectly, and many, like myself, who were ready to risk a bit to get out, but had no parlour-tricks. One had escaped from his prison-camp dressed as a German officer ; another had escaped in a dirty clothes basket, and another had been wheeled out of the camp hidden in a muck-tub ; another sportsman had painted his face green to look like a water-lily, and had swum the moat in daylight under the sentry's nose. . . . Forgery, bribery, impersonation, with an utter disregard of risks of being shot, all found their advocates in Fort 9

Thenceforth, in the book, attempts to escape are almost continuous. Captain Evans's own first effort (with two companions) was a dash over the frozen moat, followed by " a fair amount of shooting " ; a lorry-load of munition workers put an end to this. Six weeks later, with snow on the ground, he and another cut their way at night through a wired window and got away with white overclothes on, shots again following. Bad luck once more ruined their chances, and they were brought back to " a very hostile reception from a mob of angry sentries," the Feldwebel " cursing them roundly for bringing us in alive rather than dead." Several other schemes were fruitless, but at last the chance came. There were riots. A party of prisoners was dispatched by train for another camp. At a favourable moment the sentries were distracted and obstructed, Captain Evans and Lieutenant Buckley sprawled out of the window, and there began a two-hundred miles journey to the Swiss frontier. It took eighteen nights, and the description of it fills fifty very fine pages. Captain Evans returned home ; went to Palestine ; was captured by murderous Arabs and nearly killed ; made a dash for the coast alone and foodless, and failed ; was taken to Constantinople ; and got out of Turkey just before the Armistice. It is impossible to do justice to his book in a summary or in quotations. It is crowded with detail, and written in a very direct style, without ever a word put in for effect or a sentence noticeably careless. The spirit of it is equally admirable. Captain Evans has a respect for truth and his general coolness and restraint give peculiar force to his one set denunciation, which is aimed at the whole race of Turks.

Captain Evans says somewhere that he would like to know whether German prisoners here found smuggling as easy as he did. It is permissible to feel curiosity also about the escapes of Germans from prison-camps in England. Whether any of them actually got back to Germany I do not know, and I do not think we were ever told. It is not likely that many could have done so. It is one thing, prodigiously dangerous and difficult though the feat always was, to crawl, or make a midnight dash, between sentries on a land frontier ; it is another to get across the high seas. There were, I seem to remember, Germans captured in a small stolen boat, and there was one (who certainly deserved to get away) who smuggled himself on board ship, or near it, disguised as a consignment of fish or a piano, in a large wooden crate pierced with air-holes. But if none got out of the country, many escaped from their prisons, and some were at large for weeks and were recaptured after long wanderings.

Presumably some of these will have published their experiences in Germany. But as far as I know, only one such book has as yet been translated, and that was rather a thin book in which there was a short account of Donington Hall and a short, if interesting, sketch of a walk from Donington Hall to Nottingham, where the local police force interrupted the tour. Cannot some publisher get us one or two others ? It is not that one is particularly eager to hear about the domestic life of the Germans in British prison-camps, which was, to put it mildly, less eventful than that of the unfortunate English-men who fell into the hands of Germany ; though even here one would be interested to learn how English commandants and guards appeared through those strange German spectacles. But the methods of escape adopted in our own midst excite one's curiosity, and above all it would be entertaining to see how our own familiar countryside and towns and people looked to the escaping foreigner.

For the prisoner who is escaping through a strange land observes the scenes through which he passes with painful closeness and from a peculiar angle. The Germany that Captain Evans and his com-rades saw was not the Germany which the Germans saw. The moment a man was slinking on his way to the frontier the whole landscape changed. The most ordinary scenes became invested with a romantic quality. Lanes, fields, woods, cottages, rivers, bridges, signal-boxes, which were commonplace to accustomed eyes, took on a mystery, became grim and menacing, were dreaded for the perils they might conceal or blessed for their harmlessness. Every object seen was seen for the first time and in an unusual aspect ; every yokel and every dairy-maid working in the fields or walking home or chatting under a street-lamp was a possible enemy ; every enforced conversation was an adventure, and every eye was watched for the glint of suspicion. It would be an amusing thing to have a few pictures

of our own homely roads, our own streets and
railway stations, and our own routine selves,
done from the point of view of men who were
travelling across England much as though it were
an Africa, full of lurking deaths, with the courage
of solitary wanderers fighting their way out of a
region of enchantments. Did a man, four years ago,
with his heart standing still, ask the clerk at Bir-
mingham booking office, in consciously bad English,
for a ticket to Paddington ? Did a man, cold and
ragged, lie under leaves in a copse of Richmond
Park as Captain Evans lay, evening after evening,
on the hills of Bavaria ? Did one sit on the Embank-
ment watching the gulls, pretending to read a paper,
frightened of every policeman, and wondering
where to go next ? Did a party of them boil their
Bovril in the woods above Oxford ? Did stray
fugitives swim the Trent and the Thames, blunder
on the Washington Inn without knowing its name,
and see it as a sinister thing, inspect Salisbury
Cathedral, look hungrily over the moonlit Channel
from the Downs, bluff their way through com-
panies amongst whom we ourselves may have been,
take the wrong road at Guildford, and fall into a
trap at Stoke Poges ? There must be many Germans who have tales of desperate adventure in an
England which is to us so comfortable and unsus-
pecting—ending usually, no doubt, in conversations
with farmers and policemen which, and whom, they
will have found very odd.

# LORD ROSEBERY'S MISCELLANIES

IN a prefatory note to this collection Mr. John Buchan takes the responsibility for it ; he importuned Lord Rosebery to " release " his miscellaneous shorter works for publication. These include one or two long historical essays ; a few review articles and prefaces ; and a large number of disquisitions on a variety of subjects delivered from Scottish Rectorial chairs or before statues which Lord Rosebery was unveiling. How dull, were the author anybody but Lord Rosebery, it would all sound! But, the author being he, it was a collection well worth making.

The little monograph on Lord Randolph Churchill is already well known ; it is extraordinarily good, and makes one wish that Lord Rosebery would supplement it with other portraits of his contemporaries. The study of Peel is also familiar ; it is just and illuminating, and it contains a passage on the modern Prime Minister and the modern Cabinet more frank and acute than anything that has been said on the subject by any other living politician. Of the other historical papers the chief are the group which deal with Scotland. I hesitate even to touch on these arcana ; when I began reading them, so full as they are of enthusiasms and rituals and allusions strange to me, I felt almost like a shy intruder who has strayed into some service in a mosque. But they are excellent reading, and contain passages which must be an inspiration to any Scotsman who reads them. The most conspicuous of the literary essays are those on Burke and Dr. Johnson. That on Johnson was a centenary address given at Lichfield ; the main elements in the Doctor's character and in Boswell's success have never been better or more succinctly described. Lord Rosebery is devoted to these two authors above all ; but his taste, though he says little of poetry (except Burns's), and nothing of any modern author except Stevenson, is obviously catholic. He is hearty in his admirations and pleasantly candid about his dislikes. He says, refreshingly, that he finds Chesterfield's letters dreary ; he describes " The Master of Ballantrae " as an " utterly repulsive " story of " the conflict of a scoundrel against a maniac narrated by a coward " ; he betrays an intimate knowledge of Swift, Scott, and Miss Austen ; and he writes a charming appreciation of Thackeray in which the qualities and defects of " Vanity Fair " are balanced with consummate art.

Everywhere the expression is normally easy ; the periods when they come glide naturally out of the elegantly conversational. The words, as everybody knows, are admirably chosen, and the incidental jokes, often very quietly ironical, are a constant temptation to the pencil. Wordsworth " was not prone to external admiration " ; Landor would have been hard put to it to write an Imaginary Conversation between a Tory Democrat and Lord Eldon ; the old aim in Scotland was to get " two eyes for an eye and two teeth for a tooth " ; the Scotch monarch was a sort of " living Great Seal." Contemplating the developments of a mechanical age, he pictures " His Royal Highness the Prince of Wales leading home the victorious locomotive in the national race on Epsom Downs " ; he has a delicious set passage on the modern rage for memorials and testimonials ; and he frequently dwells on the drawbacks of speechifying. " Speeches," he says, in one place :

> even the best, are as evanescent as fireworks or thistle-down ; they are explored for untimely quotation during the speaker's life, and when that useful purpose ceases with his death, they cease to be opened at all ; they are even less read than old sermons, which possess an elect public of their own.

These volumes contain much wit, much sense, much sound, and much eloquent English, much interesting literary and historical criticism, many valuable studies in portraiture. Those attributes alone would give them a high rank amongst the productions of literary politicians. Except for one or two short speeches, which have no merit but a perfunctory polish, every essay and address that Lord Rosebery has compiled has displayed both wide reading and prolonged reflection. He, the most expert of ceremonial orators, has never been content that his oratory should be merely ceremonial. A man is no more on his oath in a ceremonial address than in a lapidary inscription, but Lord Rosebery has never been content to fob his audiences off with pleasant platitudes or easy first thoughts. A man with his gifts could quite easily have done it and with applause ; his mere grace of style in writing, his mere voice and gesture in speaking, were always sufficient to carry him through without trouble if he cared to be so carried through. But he always took his commissions of this kind more seriously than he thought it necessary to admit. The jesting or diffident exordium was always succeeded by the evidence of close reading and a serious desire to say something worth saying. There is hardly a paper or a speech in the collection which is not worth having for the information which it contains and the judgments based upon that information. Yet for all this the main interest of these volumes does not derive from the facts or the criticisms which they incorporate, from their varied erudition or from the admirable construction of their sentences. It is not Lord Rosebery's talent but his strain of genius which chiefly fascinates.

The quality of his imagination frequently comes out in isolated phrases or images, resembling those of his hero Burke, and of the lesser (but often Burke-like in this regard) Walter Bagehot. This is the sort of sentence I mean :—" The crises of nations, like the crises of Nature, have their thunderbolts, and Cromwell was one of these " ; and " I have seen life and death and glory chasing each other like shadows on a summer sea " ; and (to men leaving their university) " There will always be a voice from these old walls which will speak as a second conscience " ; and (when he is speaking of the swift changes in the streets and houses of London) " When in a long walk one comes on some untouched nook it is with the same surprise that one finds a patch of snow under a hedgerow in a thaw." But his imagination does not operate only in these localised flashes.

His imaginative, one may as well say poetic, frame
of mind comes out also in his power, and his constant inclination to exercise the power, of establish-
ing a sudden sympathetic contact with his audience
and compelling them to join with him in some
strange adventure of the mind. He is talking on
Burns, and he must unexpectedly, with a few words,
make his audience think of the births taking place
in the world at that instant and the possibility of
another Newton or another Cæsar being amongst
them. He is addressing the Johnsonian faithful at
Lichfield, and he startles them with the imagined
presence of Johnson lumbering into that congre-
gation and asking what the nonsense is all about.
He is talking at St. Andrews on the five hundredth
anniversary of the University, and he conjures up
the first Rector, endows him with an immortality
in the flesh, and through those conjectured eyes sees
the whole procession of events in the world during
half a millennium. He is addressing the burgesses
of Bristol on the subject of their former member
Burke, and he quotes to them Burke's words :
" What shadows we are and what shadows we pursue," with the comment that they " sum up the life
of every politician, and perhaps of every man." It
was always his habit to view the events of a generation (as a historian must) in the light of the events
of centuries and (as an imaginative artist will) the
events of centuries in the light of eternity. The pro-
cesses of time have always haunted him, and the
mysteries of human existence and human pain and
doubt. It was characteristic of him that in one of
the earliest of serious addresses, delivered to the

students of Aberdeen in 1880, he should have reminded the students, little younger than himself,
of the Dance of Death :

Day by day the horizon of human possibility,
which now lies so unbounded before you, must
contract ; the time must come when, under the
stroke of illness or the decay of nature, hope and
health, the pride and power of life and intellect,
which now seem so inseparable from your triumph-
ant youth, will have passed away.

We can confidently deduce that such reflections
were never far from him ; that they crossed his
mind at Cabinet meetings, on platforms when
thousands were cheering some joke or political
announcement, in rooms where diplomatic chaffer-
ings were proceeding over tables. This is what it
means to be of an imaginative and reflective habit ;
it is sometimes a handicap and sometimes a great
help.

Lord Rosebery says there were a hundred Glad-
stones. There may have been ; but they all got on
very happily together ; the complexity in Gladstone's heart and brain was not so great as that in
his own. Behind this book, and his other books,
and all his career, one is aware of a strange congeries
of inhabitants in that one form, the ambitious and
versatile man of affairs living with the meditative
student of mortality, the elegant and cultivated
Georgian senator with the melancholy artist of the
Romantic period. He has never paraded his more
intimate solicitudes ; on the contrary, he has desired

to preserve an exterior urbanity, to be objective in his attitude, reticent in his expression. But his temperament was always far too strongly coloured for any pride or any code of manners to be able entirely to counteract it ; it is plain that he always has been conscious of his every word and act, and, deliberately or not, his essays let us into the dominant preoccupations, temporal and eternal, of his mind. What these are may be left to the reader to discover ; but it is clear that he has always been exercised by the problem as to whether a born man of letters is ever wise in allowing himself to be swallowed up by politics.

# MINOR CAROLINES

THE third volume of Mr. Saintsbury's reprints of lesser Caroline poets was announced
before the war. The war held it up. It has now
appeared.

There is a slight distinction between it and its
predecessors. In the first two volumes the poets
were distinctly minor minors. The best of them all
was probably Katherine Philips (Orinda). The
others were mainly curiosities ; at best poets who
once or twice " came off." There was Benlowes, the
eccentric who ruined himself by benefactions to
needy poets, and whose " Theophila " was put
through the press with such unremitting assiduity
and such fluctuating intentions that scarcely any
two copies contain the same number of plates. There
was Chamberlayne, whose " Pharonnida " is an
immense narrative dunghill, in which the otherwise
unoccupied may search for, and sometimes find,
pearls. There was Chalkhill, who wrote a charming
song ; Patrick Carey, whom Sir Walter Scott
temporarily revived ; Philip Ayres, who wrote
sonnets when sonnets were not in fashion ; Kynaston
and Hall, who rose to great heights at isolated
moments ; Hannay, who is dull ; Godolphin, who
was a plaster imitation of a good poet ; and others.
But the new volume contains poets of greater stature
than these. The first three are Cleveland, Stanley,
and King.

Cleveland we may perhaps pass as not much
above the level of the others. His works were very

popular after the Restoration, because he had
lampooned the Puritans with notable offensiveness.
There are splendid bits of invective in him as there
are in his later congener, Charles Churchill ; but
he was less of a poet than Churchill, and his fame
may be greater than he deserves. Stanley and King
are far more important people. Thomas Stanley,
author of a once-celebrated " History of Philosophy,"
opulent friend and patron of half the most gifted
men of his age, was as a poet a link between Donne
and his followers and the song-writers of the Restoration. " Expectation," which begins :

> Chide, chide no more away
> The fleeting daughters of the day,
> Nor with impatient thoughts outrun
> The lazy sun.

is of the age of Herbert, but the accents of another
generation are anticipated in " The Relapse " (published 1651), which opens :

> O ! turn away those cruel eyes,
> The stars of my undoing !
> Or death in such a bright disguise
> May tempt a second wooing.

In both moods and in both measures he sometimes
got near perfection, and no general anthology of
English verse can pretend to be representative which
does not contain several of his poems. As much
may be said of Bishop King, of Chichester, who
lived from 1592 to 1669. His " Exequy on his Wife "

has often been reprinted, and can never be reprinted too often. There is no more affecting farewell in all English poetry than its closing lines :

> Sleep on, my Love, in thy cold bed
> Never to be disquieted !
> My last good night ! Thou wilt not wake
> Till I thy fate shall overtake :
> Till age, or grief, or sickness must
> Marry my body to that dust
> It so much loves ; and fill the room
> Thy heart keeps empty in thy tomb.
> Stay for me there : I will not fail
> To meet thee in that hollow vale. . . .

" The Departure," " Brave Flowers," and " Tell
Me No More " are in the same category. He is
certainly a minor poet in the light of the major poets ;
but compared to Chamberlayne or Ayres he is
gigantic. These and two others, Whiting and Flatman, are included in the new volume. The texts
have been carefully revised with the assistance of
Mr. Percy Simpson and Mr. Thom-Drury, and
the notes are as full and as racy as Mr. Saintsbury
alone could make them. It is a pleasure to see him
thumping Roundheads again in the old way. Every
page of text is welcome ; but there is one poet for
whom we may acknowledge an especial debt to
Mr. Saintsbury.

Of Cleveland there is a modern edition made by
one of those industrious American gentlemen who
write theses for the doctorate or engage themselves,
at the behest of their universities, on works of post-
graduate research. King was in the main edited by

Archdeacon Hannah eighty years ago, and Stanley's lyrics and some of his translations are accessible (though they were not when Mr. Saintsbury first planned his edition) in the edition prepared by the late Louise Imogen Guiney and published in 1907 by the late J. R. Tutin, of Hull, one of the ornaments of the English bookselling trade. All these poets are in a manner accessible, though Mr. Saintsbury's editions will certainly supersede all previous ones. Whiting and Flatman are in different case. Neither has ever been edited in modern times, and there is, I believe, no issue of either's poems later than the seventeenth century. That Whiting has not been edited I do not, after reading his works, feel surprised at. He is a lumbering narrator, with a grovelling mind and a style full of pedantry and made metaphors. He was a " character " and is amusing to meet once ; but it is likely that the English language will die out of the world before another Mr. Saintsbury arises to give him a second resurrection. But in editing Flatman (and, incidentally, unearthing several of his poems from manuscript) Mr. Saintsbury has added one more to the long series of substantial services that he has done to English poetry.

Thomas Flatman was (probably) a Norfolk man, of Winchester and New College, who was born in 1635 and died in 1688. He is the most neglected of the genuine poets of the Restoration period. Several of them still want thorough editing : Dorset, Cotton, Buckingham, Sedley, and the almost great Rochester are known to most readers of poetry only through selections in anthologies. But Flatman only just peeps into the anthologies, and even there he seems to escape notice. Except in the catalogues of Messrs. Sotheby and Hodgson—his editions are all rare and fetch large prices—I doubt if his name ordinarily appears in print once a year. Probably it is the said name that has done for his reputation ; a poet might almost as well be called John Proser, Henry Dullard, or Christopher Numskull. But he was at times a goodish poet, and one may say of him, as one can of several of his contemporaries, that had he been born in another generation he would have been a better one. He was not a consummate song-writer, but some of his songs are graceful ; and he had a particular faculty of getting touches of simplicity, of humour, and of imagination into the most pompous-looking of pindarics. It was not for nothing that one of his friends was Dr. Walter Pope, the wag who wrote that charming domestic poem, " The Old Man's Wish " ; and on the other hand Mr. Saintsbury is fully justified in saying that he is distinguished from his contemporaries by having inherited from the previous generation a constant, though not a morbid, preoccupation with Death. " No more ! Alas ! that bitter word, *No more* ! " the opening, both in sentiment and in expression, is foreign to his time. And Wordsworth himself can scarcely have written with a more simple directness than Flatman did in his " song " on the same subject :

Oh, the sad day,
When friends shall shake their heads and say
Of miserable me,

Hark! how he groans, look how he pants for breath,
See how he struggles with the pangs of Death!
When they shall say of these poor eyes,
How hollow and how dim they be!
Mark how his breast does swell and rise
Against his potent Enemy!

When some old friend shall step to my bedside,
Touch my chill face, and thence shall gently slide,
   And when his next companions say,
How does he do! What hopes? shall turn away,
   Answering only with a lift-up hand,
     Who can his fate withstand?

Flatman could not long remain at this level of
solemnity, though the solemnity was genuine. He
had to finish the poem with:

Then shall a gasp or two do more
Than e'er my rhetoric could before,
Persuade the peevish world to trouble me no more!

That whimsical note often recurs. Perhaps the
most characteristic poem of all is that in which he
very brazenly preaches his doctrine of " Anything
for a quiet life." He calls it, slightly libelling himself
in the title, " The Unconcerned," and it was written
at a time of great mundane convulsions:

Now that the world is all in a maze,
   Drums and trumpets rending heav'ns,
Wounds a-bleeding, mortals dying,
   Widows and orphans piteously crying;

Armies marching, towns in a blaze,
    Kingdoms and States at sixes and sevens ;
    What should an honest fellow do,
Whose courage, and fortunes run equally low ?
    Let him live, say I, till his glass be run,
        As easily as he may ;
Let the wine, and the sand of his glass flow to-
        gether,
    For life's but a winter's day.
        Alas ! from sun to sun,
    The time's very short, very dirty the weather,
    And we silently creep away.
Let him nothing do, he could wish undone ;
And keep himself safe from the noise of gun.

It may not be the most laudable kind of outlook,
but it is a common one, and it has seldom been so
felicitously expressed. It is reflected again in " The
Whim," which is too long to quote bodily, but of
which I may give the first stanza :

Why so serious, why so grave ?
    Man of business, why so muddy ?
Thyself from Chance thou can'st not save,
    With all thy care and study.
Look merrily then, and take thy repose ;
For 'tis to no purpose to look so forlorn,
Since the World was as bad before thou wert born,
    And when it will mend who knows ?
    And a thousand years hence 'tis all one,
If thou lay'st on a dunghill, or sat'st on a throne.

" Sit the comedy out, and that done, When the
play's at an end let the curtain fall down." All things

will be swept away by Time. " Hereafter no more thought on than my rhyme, Or faery kingdoms in Utopia." " When the puling fit of Life is gone, The worst that cruel man can do is done." He was, when writing most convincingly, something of a pessimist ; but it didn't seem greatly to upset him. He was a quiet and sensible man. In another age he might have been a religious poet, in that age he avoided the fashionable extremes of cynicism and reckless-ness. Cotton, Walton, and Pope were among his friends. Rochester jeered at him, and his reply was an eloquent and touching tribute when Rochester died.

Mr. Saintsbury has now concluded his collection. He had intended to reprint several very small writers, including Heath and Flecknoe, each of whom wrote lines of some beauty. These had to be omitted ; very likely nobody may wish to print them now. The work must have been one of immense labour, and it is difficult to realise that it is only a drop in the vast ocean of Mr. Saintsbury's production. Even now, though he is over eighty, and has vowed that his delicious " Notes on a Cellar Book " shall be his last compilation, one would not be surprised were he suddenly to undertake some new and elephantine postscript. There are certainly plenty of things left which he might profitably have done, and which it is to be hoped some later scholar with one half his enthusiasm and energy may arise to carry through. The collectors and the editors be-tween them have now fairly thoroughly sorted out and made accessible all the Elizabethans who are worth anything and all the Carolines, but our know-ledge of the Restoration, Augustan, and Georgian ages is still very imperfect. The greater poets have been edited, and it may freely be admitted that the minors of those ages are not on the same plane as their predecessors. But there is far more worth in the poetry which came between Milton and Wordsworth than is commonly allowed. The miscellanies and song books have not been explored; even so powerful a writer as Rochester has not been edited; and there are many charming poems to be routed out and assigned to their places in their authors' works. Granted the difference; but why should a hundred people know Wither's songs to one who knows Walsh's "The Despairing Lover," and why should Waller's "Go, Lovely Rose," be familiar to thousands who have never heard of Broome's scarcely less beautiful apostrophe? Jago and Cuthbert Shaw were much truer poets than Whiting or Godolphin, whom Mr. Saintsbury has considered worthy of an edition, and we can go higher than them. Who has edited John Dyer? It is into these fields that the next generation of scholars will move on. They will not find them as rich as the pastures in which Lamb and Dyce, Grosart and Bullen, ranged; but they will not find them barren. Unfortunately few of them as yet seem to have realised the direction in which they will have to move if they are to be of any service. Young students of the late seventeenth and the eighteenth centuries, who will carry on the work of Mr. Gosse, the late Austin Dobson, and the omnipresent Mr. Saintsbury, and produce editions where those men produced histories, are yet to be discovered.

# MEDIÆVAL ENGLISH POETRY

IT used to be, and to a deplorable extent still is, the fashion to say and to suppose that Chaucer (with the possible exception of Beowulf) was the only thing that mattered in English poetry before the Renaissance. Chaucer was a freak born out of time, and owing his quality largely to direct contact with French and Italian influences. There was Piers Plowman, a document. There were Hoccleve, Lydgate, and Gower, dull monks who passed their time making immense moral poems because they had nothing else to do. In John Skelton were to be found the rugged beginnings of English poetry as it has developed in the last four hundred years.

Modern research has gradually undermined this theory, and in recent years more and more of the results of exploration have been made accessible to the ordinary intelligent reader who does not care a dump for the differences between the dialects of Wessex and Mercia, and is content to let others decide for him the interesting points arising from a comparison of Text A with Text B and Text C. " Pearl " and " Gawayne and the Green Knight " are now fairly widely known ; Dunbar and Henryson have been rescued from neglect ; Richard Rolle is recognised as an important figure in the history of mysticism ; the Miracle Plays are receiving an increased amount of attention ; and, above all, the best of the mediæval lyrics have been introduced to a large public through the medium of collections such as Sir Arthur Quiller-Couch's. It would be a strong-minded anthologist who could now begin a representative book of English verse with anything later than " Sumer is a-cumin in."

Mr. Sisam's book, *Fourteenth Century Verse and Prose*, should continue the process of readjustment. He gives extracts from the work of a single century, the century of Edward II, Edward III, and Richard II. It was not perhaps the most interesting of the centuries if we consider it, as he does, with Chaucer left out. The first freshness of the spring song had died. The South (source of most of our poetry) was largely silent ; the note of the North was grim ; the misfortunes arising from war, famine, and plague bred a school of stern moralists ; the new modes of rhyme fought it out against a revival of the old alliterative blank verse. But as Mr. Sisam says, a man who reads mediæval literature without taking an interest in mediæval life is greatly handicapped ; and in the works he quotes, works almost all of artistic merit, we get much light on the life of the time— the social changes, the popular outlook, the mind of the Church, the risings and the winds of doctrine, trade, art, and the family. Gower, Wiclif, Mandeville, Barbour, Michael of Northgate, Langland : these are amongst the authors on whom he draws. His selections are excellently made, introduced and annotated. He ends with pieces from the York and Towneley plays, a few political pieces (including some of Minot's political songs), and nine miscellaneous lyrics. " Now Springs the Spray " is one of the loveliest and least known of these ; there is also a song jesting at the noise and puffing in a blacksmith's shop which is in the true line of our national humour. A more extensive view of our fourteenth century and other early lyric poetry may be obtained from the other book under review.

How great was the lyrical wealth of the Middle Ages is illustrated by the volume of Early English Lyrics compiled by Messrs. Chambers and Sidgwick. This book first appeared in 1907 ; the publication of a second impression now suggests that it has had a slow but steady sale. Its contents cover the ground from the thirteenth century to Skelton and Henry the Eighth, the advent of the sonnet with Wyatt and Surrey being regarded as the symptom of a new poetical age. We know, as Mr. Sisam says, that we can have only fragmentary remains of the lyric poetry, and especially of the secular lyric poetry, of those centuries. What we have we have only from manuscripts. Almost the only repositories of the manuscripts were monasteries. The monasteries naturally had a prejudice in favour of sober and instructive compositions. In addition to this the shorter poems, and the homelier of the longer ones, were the stock-in-trade of travelling minstrels and story-tellers, who would not have been over-anxious to disseminate their treasures in writing. Yet the contents of this volume can be compared without too disastrous a result with any volume of equal size of Elizabethan lyrics. The carols and religious poems, particularly those in praise of the Virgin, are the most numerous. They include such exquisite things as " Of a rose, a lovely rose," and " I sing of a maiden That is makeles," and " This flower is faire and fresche of hewe," which was never printed until it appeared in this book. They

include also " Quia Amore Langueo," the author
of which, were his name known, would have a great
reputation on that alone :

> In a valey of this restles minde
> > I soughte in mounteine and in mede,
> Trustinge a trewe love for to finde.
> > Upon a hill than I took hede ;
> > A voice I herde, and neer I yede,
> In huge dolour complaininge tho,
> > " See, dere soule, how my sides blede,
> Quia amore langueo."

Yet the religious poems are not, save in number,
more notable than the others. The " Nut-Brown
Maid " is one of the masterpieces of the language.
" Alison " is another. They are richly comic lyrics
like that spoken by a man concerning his wife, which
has for refrain : " I dare not seyn when she seith
' Pes,' " which, being interpreted, means " Peace."
Religion and the mystic life of mediæval England
join hands in the delicious poem which begins :

> The shepard upon a hill he satt ;
> He had on him his tabard and his hat,
> His tarbox, his pipe, and his flagat ;
> His name was called Joly Joly Wat,
> > For he was a gud herdes boy.
> > > Ut hoy !
> For in his pipe he made so much joy.

and the roots of half our nursery rhymes can be
seen in :

I have a gentil cok
  Croweth me day ;
He doth me risen erly
  My matines for to say.

I have a gentil cok ;
  Comen he is of grete ;
His comb is of red correl,
  His tail is of get.

Everywhere, by the way, new rhythms and new stanzas are to be found, the art has spontaneity but the spontaneity has art. Scarcely a lyric measure that we love to use but can be traced to these old poems. There was plenty of intelligence and plenty of ear and precisely the English feeling we know behind such a stanza as :

    Alone walking,
    In thought pleyning,
    And sore sighing,
      All desolate,
    The remembring
    Of my living,
    My deth wishing,
      Both erly and late. . . .

And there are still scores of others to mention, including the glorious spring song (1325), which begins :

    Lenten ys come with love to toune
    With blosmen and with briddes roune. . . .

## MEDIÆVAL ENGLISH POETRY

In time, presumably, we shall get the literature of the Middle Ages better in perspective. We cannot hope, unfortunately, to recover the names of the men who wrote the lyric masterpieces, and no great proportion of the lost poems is now likely to be recovered. But the historians will stop talking of Chaucer as a solitary lighthouse in a dark sea, and tiresomely recounting the names of Lydgate and Hoccleve as those of two dullards who happen to be remembered because there is nothing better to remember. But it is not easy to impress the merits of the thirteenth, fourteenth, and fifteenth centuries upon the ordinary reader, and the reason is that he will not take enough trouble—and after all why should he ?—about the language. " Love is Life," by Richard Rolle of Hampole, is a beautiful, simple and moving poem. But what is the reader who is not a scholar, or very persistent, to make of a stanza like this :

Luf es a lyght byrthen ; lufe gladdes yong and alde ;
Lufe es withowten pyne, as lofers hase me talde ;
Lufe es a gastly wyne, that makes men bygge and
    balde ;
Of lufe sale he na thyng tyne that hit in hert will
    halde.

The spelling will puzzle the reader ; he will probably think that " gastly " means " ghastly " and that " balde " means " bald," a reading which at once gives the poem a facetious air. When you add to this that some of the words are written, not as I have written them, but are sprinkled with strange

signs meaning " th," or " gh," or " g," or " y," or
" z," and that it is not always certain which of these
transliterations is intended, we have something
which seems almost as formidable to the lay eye as
would be the inscriptions of the Egyptians or the
constitution of Jugo-Slavia. Robert Mannynge of
Brunne, who flourished between 1300 and 1350, is
quoted by Mr. Sisam as explaining that he writes
simple language, without literary affectations or
elaborate versification, in order that everybody may
understand him. This is how he puts it :

> Haf I alle in myn Inglis layd
> In symple speeche as I conthe,
> That is lightest in manes mouthe.
> I mad noght for no disours,
> Ne for no seggers, no harpours,
> But for the luf of symple men
> That strange Inglis can not keen ;
> For many it ere that strange Inglis
> In ryme wate never wate it is,
> And bot thai wist what it mente,
> Alis me thought it were all schente.

It is hard luck on a man who was so determined to
be comprehensible to all that time should have
done to his verses what he deliberately abstained
from doing to them himself. But there it is : to the
ordinary reader of English literature gibberish without swarms of footnotes.

The nearest thing we can get to a remedy is
modernisation. Few modernised versions of the old
poems are likely to be as good as the originals ;

something in sense and in sound is almost sure to
be lost. Literal reprints can never be, and should
never be, superseded ; we must have the texts and
we must train the scholars. But a whole bookfull
of poems in Middle English is to most lovers of
literature a sealed bookfull. Let us regard the operation as translation (always considered permissible),
and translation of which nine-tenths of the work is
happily done in advance. Messrs. Sidgwick and
Chambers set a good example by modernising the
spelling of the later poems in their volume. There
is no reason why some other scholar, of equal taste
and practical facility, should not present us with a
large volume, containing a representative selection
of mediæval poetry, with words we understand,
ingeniously substituted for words we do not understand, and the doubtful points of metre made clear.

# MARK AKENSIDE

CENTENARY articles are rather a bore to write when everybody is writing them. On the present occasion, however, I cannot feel certain that anybody else will remember the centenary. However, here is notice to the town of Newcastle-on-Tyne and all whom it may concern. Mark Akenside, the poet, was born on November the ninth, 1721 ; and, although not as good as his friends thought him, he deserves the passing tribute of a paragraph.

He was born at Newcastle, the son of a butcher. When he was seven years old he received a wound from the paternal cleaver, as a result of which he was—like Byron and Scott it has been observed—lame for life. In 1739 he went to Edinburgh as a student of theology. He came to pray and remained to anatomise ; and in 1741 left Edinburgh as a surgeon, having printed a small volume of poems in the previous year. In London he made friends with a Mr. Dyson, a rich man, afterwards privy councillor and lord of the treasury. Dyson took a house for him and made him a handsome allowance for the rest of his life—the sort of thing that never happens to poets now. From 1746 onwards he wrote very little poetry, though he revised a good deal ; he made steady progress in his profession, wrote several medical treatises, delivered a remarkable Harveian oration, and became principal physician to Christ's Hospital. He died in 1770, aged forty-eight, and his poems were collected after his death by Dyson and issued in 1772 in a handsome form.

# MARK AKENSIDE

Akenside's poems, like those of most of his best contemporaries, are not véry voluminous. They fill three hundred smallish pages in the Aldine edition of his works, which is the best edition and contains an excellent memoir by Dyce. There are the two versions of " The Pleasures of the Imagination " ; there are thirty-three Odes, nine Inscriptions, " The Epistle to Curio," and fewer than a dozen other poems. In his own day he had a very great reputation. When he first appeared in London the manuscript of " The Pleasures " was shown by Dodsley to the dying Pope, who urged its publication on the grounds that its author (then only twenty-two, we should remember) was " no everyday writer."

The public agreed, and for the rest of his life, and, indeed, until the end of the century, Akenside was ranked with the important English poets. A few very detached and wary people realised that he was not quite deserving of that. Gray said of the long poem that it was " above the middling," and that some of the descriptive parts were very good, but that it was often obscure, unintelligible, and loaded with philosophical jargon ; as for the critics, he remarked that poems might just as well be judged by " the ladies that keep the bars " in the coffee houses as by them. Horace Walpole refers to him contemptuously as " another of these tame geniuses, a Mr. Akenside, who writes odes," and Dr. Johnson mingled his praise with censure in a very characteristic way. Akenside had possessed " an unnecessary and outrageous zeal for what he called and thought liberty . . . an impetuous eagerness to subvert and confound, with very little care what shall be established." Akenside was also one of what Johnson called " the brethren of the blank song "; he employed blank verse which Johnson disliked as betraying " luxuriant and active minds into such self-indulgence that they pile image upon image, ornament upon ornament, and are not easily persuaded to close the sense at all." When Johnson condemns him he does it with a relish which he could not help feeling when thumping a Radical. When Akenside is lyrical he talks of him " laying his ill-fated hand upon his harp." " Of his Odes," he says in his " Life," " nothing favourable can be said "; and in conversation his comment on the publication of a Collected Akenside was : " One bad ode may be suffered, but a number of them together makes one sick." Nevertheless, he thought ultimately that Akenside was a better poet than Gray, and for all his criticism (acute as always) of detail, he said that Akenside's longest poem showed "great felicity of genius," and that he had written blank verse better than most people.

The generality went farther ; the " Ode to the Naiads " was perhaps the most highly esteemed short poem of its age, and it was not an obscure or absurd contemporary who depicted Akenside in heaven with Plato and Virgil weaving chaplets for him and Lucretius and Pindar retiring modestly behind. Up to 1820, and later, no collection of the poets was complete without him, but the Romantic movement completely obscured him. He had none of those attributes which were once more looked for in poetry : strong passion, novel music, direct

or vivid language, mysticism, sensuousness. The
intellectual element in him was the strongest ; his
verse, whatever might be said for or against it, was
felt to be the very type of that stiffness, that poly-
syllabic orotundity, that artificiality of image, against
which the new poets revolted. He was more and
more relegated to the histories. Even Mr. Saintsbury finds nothing good in him except the satirical
" Epistle to Curio," and to most modern readers he
is merely a name, and supposed to be a dull dog,
no more and no less unreadable than Armstrong or
the dozens of couplet-writers and ode-mongers who
flourished at the same time. He is, it is thought,
merely a cold confectioner, a moral platitudinarian,
whose work may safely be neglected.

He will never stand again where he did. But if he
be read for what he can give and not for what he
cannot give, less contempt may be felt for those who
once hailed him as a great genius. The man who
wrote " The Pleasures of the Imagination " may
have been a prig, and rather chilly ; but he was no
fool, and there was beyond question a poet in him.
The synopses to the books are certainly enough to
make most modern readers take to their heels. His
object, he says, is, " by exhibiting the most engaging
prospects of nature, to enlarge and harmonise the
imagination, and by that means insensibly dispose
the minds of men to a similar taste and habit of
thinking in religion, morals, and civil life " ; and
his verses are introduced with summarising sentences
such as " The separation of the works of Imagination from Philosophy, the cause of their abuse among
the moderns. Prospect of their reunion under the

influence of public Liberty." He was a severe young man, and a young man with a system. Moreover, he could be guilty of the worst eighteenth-century excesses in pomposity and sham decoration. The stock epithets are everywhere, and the abstractions : his didacticism is grave and his imagery rather stiff even in his best passages. It is amusing to find lines of his which can be paralleled from the Romantics. Where Shelley writes :

> Liquid Peneus was flowing
> And all dark Tempe lay

Akenside puts it :

> Where, gliding through his daughter's honored shades,
> The smooth Peneus from his glassy flood
> Reflects purpureal Tempe's pleasant scene.

The adjectives are confusing, and Shelley is unmistakably better. Where Keats writes :

> Beauty is Truth, Truth Beauty, that is all. . . .

Akenside's version is :

> For Truth and Good are one,
> And Beauty dwells in them and they in her,
> With like participation.

This we recognise as too complicated and prosy in expression. The fact remains that Akenside's imagination was struck by the scenes, and that Akenside's intellect entertained the ideas. Grant him the rather monumental style, and many eloquent, beautiful, and interesting things will be found in this work of a precocious youth. Sometimes he even stumbles on a simple and direct line, as in the end of the passage where he says he is exploring the intellectual abyss to gather a laurel culled :

Where never poet gained a wreath before,

and passages dignified and moving, in spite of an occasional redundancy, are plentiful. Here are several :

Say, why was man so eminently raised
Amid the vast Creation ? why ordained
Through life and death to dart his piercing eye,
With thoughts beyond the limit of his frame ?
But that the Omnipotent might send him forth,
In sight of mortal and immortal powers,
As on a boundless theatre, to run
The great career of justice ; to exalt
His generous aim to all diviner deeds ;
To shake each partial purpose from his breast ;
And through the mists of passion and of sense,
And through the tossing tide of chance and pain,
To hold his course unfaltering. . . .

Now amazed she views
The empyreal waste, where happy spirits hold,
Beyond this concave heaven, their calm abode,
And fields of radiance, whose unfading light
Has travelled the profound six thousand years,
Nor yet arrives in sight of mortal things.

> On my strain,
> Perhaps even now, some cold, fastidious judge
> Casts a disdainful eye ; and calls my toil,
> And casts the love and beauty which I sing,
> The dream of folly.  Thou, grave censor ! say,
> Is beauty then a dream, because the glooms
> Of dulness hang too heavy on thy sense
> To let her shine upon thee ? So the man
> Whose eye ne'er opened on the light of heaven,
> Might smile with scorn while raptured vision tells
> Of the gay-coloured radiance flushing bright
> O'er all creation.

If this last passage is not early Keats, in feeling and expression, I should like to know what it is. The last thing I am going to do is to claim Akenside as one more precursor of the Romantic Revival ; but he at least had something in common with the romantic poets. The peroration of " The Pleasures," in which God is seen behind " the winds and rolling waves, the sun's unwearied course, the elements and seasons " is reminiscent of Wordsworth in expression if the philosophy is Wordsworth's with a difference.

Gray said that Akenside's great work was published nine years too soon. This meant that Akenside would develop. He did not, and the springs of poetry almost dried up in him. There is charm and sense in several of the Odes, such as the " Hymn to Cheerfulness," beginning :

> How thick the shades of evening close !
> How pale the sky with weight of snows !
> Haste, light the tapers, urge the fire,
> And bid the joyless day retire.

" Amoret " is deliciously neat, and so is " The Complaint," and the " Ode to the Evening Star " is one of the sweetest lyrics of the century. Its opening :

> To night retired, the queen of heaven
> With young Endymion stays. . . .

is perfect, and the poem very nearly lives up to it. The description of the nightingale at the wood's edge would bear comparison with any other that exists. Here is one stanza :

> Hark, how through many a melting note
> She now prolongs her lays :
> How sweetly down the void they float !
> The breeze their magic path attends ;
> The stars shine out ; the forest bends ;
> The wakeful heifers gaze.

There are happy touches in even the worst of the shorter poems, and " The Epistle to Curio," an onslaught against Pulteney, whom he regarded as a renegade, has a formal finish and a fierce sincerity which are lacking from the livelier satires of Charles Churchill. Akenside was not a great poet, but the revival of interest in Dyer should be extended to him also.

Akenside's character is not very favourably depicted by his biographers. Only from one or two of his poems can it be deduced that he was ever in love ; he became, whatever he was when young, a stiff and formal bachelor, vain, dogmatic, inclined to lose his temper if he were opposed, an obstinate theologian and a peppery radical. Smollett lampooned him in "Peregrine Pickle," and the most startling stories were told about his brutality to the poor patients at Christ's Hospital :

> If the poor affrighted patients did not return a direct answer to his queries, he would often discharge them from the hospital. He evinced a particular disgust to females, and generally treated them with harshness. It was stated that this moroseness was occasioned by disappointment in love.

Thus the world saw him, and his character was thought to be suited to his appearance—the pale face, the rigid figure, the precise, elegant clothes, the long sword and hobbling gait. But the sensibility and fancy which are visible in his poems coloured his conversation when among his intimates ; his eloquence, when he got going, was very impressive ; and his scholarship has been excelled by few English poets.

# WILLIAM COLLINS

THE bi-centenary of the birth of William Collins occurred last week ; he was born on Christmas Day, 1721. In various quarters timely tributes were paid to his memory. I should have written about Collins had I written at all last week. I feel some doubt as to the chances of my being here when his next centenary arrives, and I take the liberty of coming in a week after the fair.

The elements of Collins's biography are few and well known. He was born on December 25, 1721, at Chichester, where his father, a hatter, was twice Mayor. In 1733 he went to Winchester, where he was a friend of Joseph Warton, and wrote a good deal of verse. In 1740 he went to Queen's College, Oxford, and in 1741 was elected a Demy at Magdalen. Next year, while still under twenty-one, he published his " Persian Eclogues," which he had begun at school. He failed to obtain a fellowship, left Oxford because of his debts, came into a legacy, and squandered it in excesses in London. He contemplated entering the Church and the Army ; his uncle, Colonel Martin, said he was " too indolent even for the army." At twenty-five he published his " Odes," which brought him the friendship of Thomson ; at twenty-seven his uncle, the Colonel, left him a small competency and he retired to Chichester. His " Ode on the Popular Superstitions of the Highlands " dates from 1750. Nothing later survives. Collins lived nine years more, but they were years of melancholy and intermittent madness. He died at thirty-seven and a half, having passed clean out of the sight of literary London, which nowhere recorded his death.

Less than two thousand verses by Collins survive. The number would be slightly larger did we possess everything he is known to have written. He published at Winchester two poetical pamphlets of which no copies are believed to exist, and at the end of his productive career an " Ode on the Greek Theatre," which may have ranked with his finest works. But it would be a small volume at best ; fertility was not a characteristic of the poets of the eighteenth century, especially the best poets, who may be supposed to have been cramped by the " correct " spirit of the time. Collins's poems are few, and his good poems are very few indeed. Any student of literary history must be struck by the iteration with which critics quote the same few pieces by him over and over again. They quote, and they must quote, the first stanza of the perfect " Dirge in Cymbeline " :

> To fair Fidele's grassy tomb
>> Soft maids and village hinds shall bring
> Each opening sweet, of earliest bloom
>> And rifle all the breathing Spring.

They quote again the stanza, anticipatory of Gray's " Elegy," in the unrhymed " Ode to Evening " :

> Now Air is hush'd, save where the weak-ey'd Bat,
> With short shrill Shriek flits by on leathern Wing.
> Or where the Beetle winds
> His small but sullen Horn.

They quote, too, some part of " How Sleep the Brave who Sink to Rest " :

> By fairy hands their knell is rung ;
> By forms unseen their dirge is sung ;
> There honour comes, a pilgrim grey,
> To deck the turf that wraps their clay ;
> And freedom shall awhile repair,
> To dwell, a weeping hermit there.

They commend the " Ode to Pity," they admire the " Ode to the Passions," and they find in the " Ode on the Popular Superstitions of the Highlands of Scotland " the germs of a great deal of later poetry. Beyond these they find little to praise ; they seldom even bother to hunt for excellent lines in the " Eclogues."

The volume of Collins's good work, then, is very small. Its quality, however, has, by general consent, given him a high place among the secondary English poets. And the peculiar merits ascribed to him are his occasional technical perfection, his beautiful touches of Nature, and his position as " a forerunner of the romantic movement." When reading dissertations on this last matter, and speculations as to what Collins would have done had he been born in another age, I sometimes wonder whether we may not perhaps be in danger of losing our sense of proportion about him. He was certainly a fine craftsman ; he had a fastidious ear and was an indefatigable corrector of epithets ; he sometimes struck off a phrase or a stanza of classic perfection. But there is little sign in his external form of a revolt against the conventions of his contemporaries, little ground for holding that he was, like Blake, or like Christopher Smart, demonstrably born out of due time ; and the more we examine the poetic undergrowth of the age the less importance shall we attach to the natural images of which so much has been made. To the Leigh Hunt circle the whole eighteenth century was bare of natural images ; the regularity of the eighteenth-century forms and the conventionality of the eighteenth-century language acted as a crust which prevented these enthusiasts in revolt from seeing anything at all alive behind it. Later critics tended to adopt the same view, partly because of sheer ignorance of eighteenth-century work. In our own time the eighteenth century is being gradually re-examined, and particularly with a view to discovering natural images. The result is that traces of direct contact with nature are continually being found in unexpected or obscure quarters. Dyer's " Grongar Hill " has been rediscovered ; there has been a turn of the tide in favour of Thomson ; the search is made not entirely without success even in Young and Akenside ; and we may expect to find in the near future that extracts from Scott, Shaw, Cunningham, and others will be added to the growing list of examples proving that there were always souls who revolted against the prevalent habit of concealing strong emotion, and the prevalent refusal to look straight at natural beauty and describe what one saw and felt in simple language.

Collins's historical eminence has partly been due to overmuch levelling of the surrounding country.

## WILLIAM COLLINS

The Georgian age was certainly not as great poetically as the ages before and after it ; but, with all its artificiality and prosiness, it was not quite so barren as it used to be thought, and Gray and Collins were not such sports—though they were undoubtedly the finest artists of their times—as they used to be thought. Suppose Collins had written this :

> Swiftly from the mountain's brow,
>   Shadows, nurs'd by night, retire :
> And the peeping sun-beam, now,
>   Paints with gold the village spire.
>
> Philomel forsakes the thorn,
>   Plaintive where she prates at night ;
> And the Lark, to meet the morn,
>   Soars beyond the shepherd's sight.
>
> From the low-roof'd cottage ridge,
>   See the shatt'ring swallow spring ;
> Darting through the one-arch'd bridge,
>   Quick she dips her dappled wing.

If Collins had written that—even though it be not quite so neat as his neatest—it would be a stock illustration of his position as a " precursor " of Wordsworth and the rest of them. It is from John Cunningham's " Day," and a hundred other mid-eighteenth-century poems, examples of close observation and fresh feeling, could be found.

As a matter of fact that seems to me fresher than anything in Collins ; I will go farther and say that

Collins does not seem to me a signal example of a man born out of due time. On the contrary he seems to me to have been on fairly good terms with the eighteenth-century conventions. His learning, his personifications, his smoothness do not appear as things occasional or things against which he was rebelling. His finest passages, unlike those in " The Song to David," do not read like passages written in another century; they are rather the perfect flower of eighteenth-century formalism; he was a genuine poet, but a poet of the grave, discreet and scholarly kind, whose transports would always have been moderate and who would always have inclined to the less buoyant measures. It is a lovely passage in the " Ode to Evening " about the " hamlets brown and dim-discovered spires "; it shows him a true poet, but not necessarily an untimely romantic; and he proceeds at once, without apparent discomfort, to

> While sallow autumn fills thy lap with leaves,
> Or winter, yelling thro' the troublous air,
> Affrights thy shrinking train,
> And rudely rends thy robes.

And nobody compelled him to furnish his poems with historical and linguistic notes. He was, as a writer, slightly touched with frigidity, and it was not a frigidity imposed from outside. There is certainly no contradiction to this in the description of him given by his first editor, Langhorne. I will quote this in full, as it seems to me rather to confirm what I have been saying :

# WILLIAM COLLINS

Mr. Collins was, in stature, somewhat above the middle size ; of a brown complexion, keen, expressive eyes, and a fixed, sedate aspect, which from intense thinking, had contracted an habitual frown. His proficiency in letters was greater than could have been expected from his years. He was skilled in the learned languages, and acquainted with the Italian, French and Spanish. It is observable that none of his poems bear the marks of an amorous disposition, and that he is one of those few poets, who have sailed to Delphi, without touching at Cythera. The allusions of this kind that appear in his " Oriental Eclogues " were indispensable in that species of poetry ; and it is very remarkable that in his " Passions," an ode for music, love is omitted, though it should have made a principal figure there.

Thomson, Warton and Langhorne were Collins's poetical friends. They were all of the eighteenth century. Warton was distinctly more " romantic " in proclivity than Collins ; unfortunately he was not so good.

# HERMAN MELVILLE

THE reputation of Herman Melville has had curious vicissitudes. Seventy years ago, for a brief period, he was widely known on both sides of the Atlantic. After " Moby Dick " he lapsed into a semi-obscurity which lasted for the remaining forty years of his life. New editions of his principal works came out at rare intervals ; now and again some writer peculiarly interested in the sea —Stevenson, Clark Russell, and, later, Mr. Masefield—celebrated his genius ; periodic attempts were made by critics who had come across him to induce a wide public to read him. But his death in 1891 was almost unnoticed, and for nearly thirty years after that he continued to be what he had been—to the few a great classic, to the many barely a name. And when I say the many I mean not the greater many, but the many who are in the habit of reading good books. Some strange inhibition seems to have operated. You could tell an intelligent man about Melville ; he might remark that somebody else had told him about Melville ; and he would then go away and leave Melville unread. Possibly Melville's titles—" Typee," " Omoo," " Moby Dick "—may have had something to do with it. At any rate, there it was. In 1919 Melville's centenary was celebrated ; that is to say, it occurred. The last two years have seen articles, and good articles, about him in most of the leading critical journals ; the Oxford Press has reissued " Moby Dick " precisely as the author wrote it ; and now an American enthusiast, with the help of family papers, has compiled a biography. Can we hope that these latest attempts to incorporate Melville in the list of authors with whom every reading person must have some familiarity will be more successful ? Possibly what seems like a curse may still be in operation ; but here at least is one more effort.

Herman Melville was born in New York in 1819, of good Colonial stock. His maternal grandfather was a Dutch Revolutionary General ; on his father's side he sprang from the Scotch Melvilles. At eighteen he took a trip to Liverpool and back as cabin boy on a merchantman ; the experience was a cruel one. After a brief engagement as a schoolmaster he went to sea again, and lived for three years the life which was the substance of all his finest works. He began with a whaling cruise under a brutal captain. He deserted in the Marquesas, lived for several months with charming cannibals in a valley like Eden, escaped (after killing a one-eyed chieftain with a boat-hook) ; went another cruise and was involved in a mutiny at Tahiti ; spent some time in the French prison there ; and wound up with two long cruises in a United States frigate. The details of his adventures, both at sea and in the islands, were in the highest degree remarkable. Evil fortune persecuted him ; his character and his courage invariably rescued him, in the most melodramatic way, at the moment of extremity. Two incidents from his homeward voyage may be quoted. Through no fault of his own, he omitted to perform some duty on the frigate ; he was already lashed to the grating for a flogging when, with unparalleled but successful impertinence, a corporal of marines (who had never heard of " Pinafore ") spoke up for him to thè captain and got him released. He was almost within sight of home when he went aloft to reeve the stun'-sail halyards. His jacket was pitched over his head, and he fell a hundred feet into the sea. " So protracted did my fall seem, that I can even now recall the wondering how much longer it would be ere all was over, and I struck." He thought himself dead. " But of a sudden some fashionless form brushed my side—some inert, coiled fish of the sea ; the thrill of being alive again tingled in my nerves, and the strong shunning of death shocked me through." He was picked up, and in ten minutes was sent aloft again to complete the uncompleted task. The whole episode is marvellously described in " White Jacket," the book which secured the abolition of flogging in the U.S. Navy.

The end of this voyage, the story of which concludes whilst land is still out of sight (" I love an indefinite infinite background, a vast, heaving, rolling, mysterious rear "), marks the end of Melville's active life. He was twenty-five. He married and brought up a family, he made two trips to Europe (writing full and amusing diaries, which are reprinted by Mr. Weaver), he had a short stimulating friendship with Hawthorne. By the time he was forty he had written all the most important of his books. For the rest of his life he was externally a customs officer, of whom the world became increasingly oblivious, and his inner life was that of an imaginative philosopher, whose writings were scattered with obscure splendours and speculations of terrifying sombreness. A few people knew him as a bronzed and bearded recluse who had had a rather disreputably violent past and now read Kant and Plato. They might think what they chose. He felt himself to be growing perpetually, but he ceased to be very much interested in what others thought of him. " I have come to regard this matter of fame as the most transparent of all vanities. I read Solomon more and more, and every time see deeper and deeper and unspeakable meanings in him."

What could be more pessimistic, more disillusioned ? It certainly would be impossible to describe Melville as anything but a pessimist. He habitually faced the harshest facts in the universe ; they hurt him, and he had no explanation for them. Looking for an image of his attitude when in contemplation one thinks inevitably of the gentle and meditative mate Starbuck, looking over the side of the " Pequod" as she floats over the silken sunlit Pacific, and thinking of the world of horror under that lovely surface, the perpetual massacre, the vile writhing shapes, the ruthless rows of teeth. The whole book—and " Moby Dick " is quintessential Melville as well as the crown of his artistic achievement—has been resolved into an allegory of despair. The mad captain, Ahab, sleeplessly chasing the great White Whale, who had mutilated him, is that innermost ego to the nature and insistence of which Melville so often recurs. The mates, quiet Starbuck, and jovial Stubb, and commonplace Flask, are the recurrent moods with which he must keep company. The chase is the chase of life, the thing hunted an invulnerable brutality and an inevitable defeat. Again and again the theme is directly and openly returned to ; the eternal problem of evil is posed in all its manifestations ; sentences and pages are written which momentarily open black abysses of despair or present to the mind with irresistible force pictures of nightmare horror. No writer could more powerfully convey such pictures to the imagination ; none has exceeded Melville in the gift of using a single word or phrase which stabs the heart and leaves it throbbing with dread. Whenever Moby Dick is seen he seems " the gliding great demon of the seas of life." Ahab, momentarily softening to the poor black boy, Pip, speaks to him of " omniscient gods oblivious of suffering man ; and man, though idiotic, and knowing not what he does, yet full of the sweet things of love and gratitude." Consider, says the author, the eternal wars of the sea :

> Consider all this ; and then turn to this green, gentle, and most docile earth ; consider them both, the sea and the land ; and do you not find a strange analogy to something in yourself ? For as this appalling ocean surrounds the verdant land, so in the soul of man there lies one insular Tahiti, full of peace and joy, but encompassed by all the horrors of the half-known life. God keep thee ! Push not off from that isle, thou canst never return.

Melville himself pushed off ; at least in the sense that he became lost in speculation. Perhaps it was inevitable, as Miss Meynell suggests in her excellent little introduction to the new edition, that this should

happen to the author of " Moby Dick." There are
depths so great that if the diver reaches them he
sinks to return no more. But in " Moby Dick "
itself, the struggles of the intellect with the enigma
are not yet out of the control of the artist ; moreover, one is liable to give a false impression in saying
that the book is pessimistic. It has nothing in common
with the grey miseries of the enfeebled. Its darkest
passages are passionate in the writing and produce
an exhilaration in the reader ; both the glory as
well as the awfulness of life are celebrated at white
heat ; and the moods of the book are as varied as
the " Pequod's " crew. The jovial Stubb and the
matter-of-fact Flask get their turns with Starbuck
and the captain. Every variety of marine experience,
all the beauty and terror of the South Seas, a world
of human character and lively external incident, are
here. At one moment we are watching a bloody fight
on deck, at another listening to a story in a café at
Lima, at another boiling down whale-blubber in
the fire-lit night ; there are enough battles and
storms and encounters to make a dozen books for
boys. Not only does one feel that there was a Conrad
and a Stevenson in Melville, but frequently one is
forcibly reminded, in chapters at a time, of Dickens
and Defoe. How could a book open more briskly
and humorously and excitingly ? In what novel can
one find a record of fact so elaborate, a collection of
odd learning so amusing and peculiar, as in that
large section of the book which describes the whole
history, structure, and fate of the whale, and epito-
mises the manners and customs of whalers ?

Melville's laugh is as loud as his brooding is deep,

and no recorder of the surface of life ever had a keener eye for every kind of detail or a more retentive memory. And the whole wealth of his passion and knowledge, humour and suffering is poured out in language which is at its best unsurpassed, and in a curious mixed form—plain narrative is broken up by essays, treatises, dramatic dialogues—which superbly justifies itself.

He lapsed sometimes into excesses of rhetoric ; his love for Sir Thomas Browne sometimes betrayed him ; but he equalled Browne's sentences and De Quincey's apostrophes when he was thinking of neither, and none of his numerous South Sea successors has approached him in the power of natural description. " I will add," he says, when discussing ropes, " that Manilla is much more handsome and becoming to the boat than Hemp. Hemp is a dusky, dark fellow, a sort of Indian ; but Manilla is a golden-haired Circassian to behold." " For," he says in parentheses, " there is an æsthetics in all things." That there was to him, that he was a born poet, is evident everywhere—except sometimes in his poetry. Imagery pours out of him, and everything he mentions is touched with light. I should like to reprint the whole marvellous chapter on " The Whiteness of the Whale " ; I can only quote a few poor sentences to illustrate his qualities :

The subterranean miner that works in us all, how can one tell whither leads his shaft by the ever-shifting, muffled sound of his pick ?

Few are the foreheads, which, like Shakespeare's or Melanchthon's, rise so high, and descend so low, that the eyes themselves seem clear, eternal, tideless mountain lakes ; and all above them, in the forehead's wrinkles, you seem to track the antlered thoughts descending there to drink, as the Highland hunters track the snowprints of the deer.

To any meditative Magian rover, this serene Pacific, once beheld, must ever after be the sea of his adoption. It rolls the midmost waters of the world, the Indian Ocean and Atlantic being but its arms. The same waves wash the moles of the new-built Californian towns, but yesterday planted by the recentest race of men, and lave the faded but still gorgeous skirts of Asiatic lands, older than Abraham ; while all between float milky-ways of coral isles, and low-lying, endless, unknown archipelagoes, and impenetrable Japans. Thus this mysterious, divine Pacific zones the world's whole bulk about ; makes all coasts one bay to it ; seems the tide-beating heart of earth. Lifted by these eternal swells, you needs must own the seductive god, bowing your head to Pan.

But few thoughts of Pan stirred Ahab's brain, as standing like an iron statue at his accustomed place beside the mizzen rigging, with one nostril he unthinkingly snuffed the sugary musk from the Bashee isles (in whose sweet woods mild lovers must be walking), and with the other consciously inhaled the salt breath of the new-found sea ; that sea in which the hated White Whale must even then be swimming. Launched at length upon these almost final waters, and gliding towards the Japanese cruising-ground, the old man's purpose intensified itself. His firm lips met like the lips of a vice ; the Delta of his forehead's veins swelled like overladen brooks ; in his very sleep, his ringing cry ran through the vaulted hull, " Stern all ! the White Whale spouts thick blood ! "

There have been more profuse great writers than Melville, and, as some may think, wiser men ; but I do not believe that there exists a greater work of prose fiction in English than " Moby Dick."

# STOCK PHRASES

M R. A. M. HYAMSON is known to amateurs of lexicography as the compiler of an extremely useful small " Dictionary of Universal Biography." His latest work, *A Dictionary of English Phrases*, should be equally useful. Much of the information he gives will be found in existing dictionaries of quotations and of " Phrase and Fable," but he has worked on a rather eclectic plan of his own with a view to providing a complement to the ordinary verbal dictionary. He himself says that he has included, besides " phrases proper," " phraseological and historical allusions," " catchwords " (political and other), " stereotyped modes of speech," " metaphorical clichés," " corrupted words," " nicknames and sobriquets," " derivations from personal names," " quotations that have become part of the language," " war words," etc. It is a curious company ; but I think that experience will prove that Mr. Hyamson's method justifies itself.

A large part of any such work must be devoted to telling the instructed reader what he knows already. You cannot compile dictionaries with a single eye on those who least need them. Many of us may not need to be told the meaning and origin of Gordian Knot, Rump Parliament, Gradgrind, Procrustean Bed, or the Seven Ages of Man. A very large number of the purchasers of this book will probably never have need to refer to

Goth, A : a barbarian ; one heedless of the claims of the arts and sciences. After the people that overran and devastated the Roman Empire in the third and fifth centuries.

Yet he would be a very learned man who should find any page on which there was no information which was novel to him ; and I myself, not having an entire issue of this journal at my disposal, can only give a few specimens to indicate the sort of material which Mr. Hyamson supplies.

Oddly, the very first phrase which caught my eye when I opened the book was one which comes from a source that I had not dreamed of suspecting. " Not worth a twopenny damn " is the phrase ; it looks too simple to invite curiosity ; but according to our present authority it derives from the fact that there was " an Indian coin, a dam, which much depreciated in value." Opposite it I noticed " uncle" as used of a pawnbroker. It comes, apparently, from the Latin *uncus*, a hook on which pledges used to be hung. There is no mistaking the meaning of " The Great Unwashed," which appears just below " Uncle," but a very small fraction of those who employ this offensive designation will know that it was first used by Edmund Burke. " Go to Bath " is said to be in allusion to the popularity of Bath as a place for the treatment of lunatics ; but " Go to Jericho " is disputed. Some will derive it from the fact that Henry VIII used a country place called Jericho as a retreat ; others from King David's order to certain people to go to Jericho until their beards were grown. King David : " as drunk as David's sow." Looking that up I find it amidst " drunk as a cobbler," " drunk as a fiddler,"

" drunk as a lord," " drunk as a pope," " drunk as the devil," and " drunk as a tinker at Banbury." It is alleged that there was a man David Lloyd, of Hereford, whose wife was found drunk in a pig-stye when he took a party to see a sow he owned. It isn't very convincing, but nothing better offers. " To let the cat out of the bag " is attributed to a custom of selling cats in bags, falsely representing the same to be sucking-pigs.

The " Ashes " (cricketing) have been satisfactorily run down to the *Sporting Times* of 1882. Of " chaff," meaning banter, three explanations are offered, one of which is that there was

> a custom in the North Midlands of emptying a sack of chaff at the door of a man who ill-treats his wife, to indicate that thrashing is done there.

" Chestnut " (an old joke) is variously attributed ; I am surprised to find it so modern that it can plausibly be traced to a story of a chestnut farm too frequently told by E. A. Abbey, the painter, who died as recently as 1911. " To face the music " has no fewer than four suggested derivations :

> From (1) the actor, who in facing the music faces his public, his critics ; (2) the difficulty in training army horses to remain quiet in the company of a regimental band ; (3) the drumming out of men dismissed by the U.S. army ; (4) the muster of militia-men who are drawn up in ranks facing the band.

You take your choice ; but with such uncertainty one feels that the genuine original context may have been none of these. The mention of the actor facing his public sends me in search of another phrase. It is here, but only in the form of " To get the big bird " ; Mr. Hyamson should note " to get the bird " as the commoner variant. Amongst terms which are less commonly used than they might be, I notice " Albino Poets," which was used by Wendell Holmes of the sicklier kind of bards.

It is inconceivable that such a collection should be complete, or that a collection in one volume should not frequently disappoint the reader. Granted that it contains any considerable amount of information which is new to one and not easily accessible elsewhere, one ought to be grateful for it. I certainly, to use a phrase which, as I now learn, derives from Heywood's " Proverbes " (1546), will not look the gift-horse in the mouth. Mr. Hyamson himself, in fact, disarms criticism in his very modest preface. He does not profess to be able exactly to define the scope of his book ; he seems to have been guided as much by intuition as by reason. He says that critics who point out deficiencies will seldom lack justification, and he asks for suggestions for additional entries. For myself, I think that it would be worth his while to pay rather more attention to slang, and especially to well-established American slang, which is in continual process of naturalisation here. He has plenty of mid-Victorian words and phrases which came from America : " carpet-bagger," " bunkum," " bark up the wrong tree," and hundreds of others. But if he went freely about London with his ears pricked up (Virgil's " Aeneid I." and Chapman's " All Foole's Day "), he would certainly encounter many more recent immigrants. We may never adopt the admirable word " copper-throat," for we are already so well-stocked with terms descriptive of drinking propensities. Possibly " rubber-neck," also, dear to all students of O. Henry, who reduced it to " rube," may fail to get a home here. But "beat it" is coming, "beat the band " is already popular, and " to go on the water-wagon " (briefly, on the wagon) may be heard almost anywhere. Mr. Hyamson would find it easy to make room for many additions if he could bring himself —though the process must be distressing to any dictionary-maker—to leave out some of the phrases he has now thought fit to include. Some of the solemner nicknames might go. It is quite right that we should be told that " The British Solomon " was James I ; the phrase has long been widely current, and is often used without explanation in the context. But it is hardly worth while to record the fact that a forgotten painter was at one time known as " the English Salvator Rosa." There are other words—" uppertendom " is an instance—which are merely awkward attempts at coinage which have definitely failed. And the words made from proper names might be diminished. I see " Beardsleyism " here, defined as :

A pictorial illustration in black-and-white in the style of Aubrey Vincent Beardsley.

The word has doubtless been used, but it is unlikely to be used if or when Beardsley has been forgotten. Anybody can make that sort of word at any moment ;

it defines itself. We are quite likely to see Lloyd-Georgism, Carsonism, Byronism, Conradism, Wilsonism, and many other such in the papers to-morrow morning.

These are small suggestions. I turn from the book with a certain melancholy. Why ? Because of the number of fine phrases it contains which we use daily and the fineness of which we never realise. It is a cemetery of dead metaphors ; these were lovely and pleasant in their lives, and in death they are put into dictionaries. Surely the reflection is a little saddening. A man may make an image which is of local application or a little above the heads of mankind, and it will retain its freshness in perpetuity. Let him do the best thing of all—make an image which is widely applicable and plain to the common understanding—and his beautiful creation will be killed by too much handling. What an agreeable shock of surprise must have been felt by those who were first told by an imaginative man that they were looking for a needle in a bundle of hay ! With us familiarity has bred blindness ; we drop the phrase out without seeing any needle or any hay. " To build on the sand," " to beat the air," " to sponge," " to split hairs," " to feather one's nest "—there are a thousand of them in this book. They have become so worn by usage that we might almost as well be without them ; they are said to " enrich the language," but the only person who really gets full enjoyment out of this opulence is a foreigner who learns English. Every great writer contributes to the stock ; his very best phrases are withdrawn from him and turned into half-obliterated currency.

# STOCK PHRASES

And for us there comes ready to our tongue a stock description of every situation and a stock comparison for every quality. " Straight—as a die," " Old—as the hills," " Soft—as a peach," " Raining—like cats and dogs," " Dark—as pitch " ; half the epithets we have bring their little withered tails behind them with scarcely a wag left in them. " A Dictionary of English Phrases " is an immense mausoleum full of the mummies of Samsons, and Helens, and Cleopatras.

# THE LAUREATES

MR. E. K. BROADUS'S scholarly and amusing book, *The Poets Laureate in England*, contains a study of the origins of the laureateship, a history of its development as a regular institution, sketches of the lives of the Laureates, and accounts of their work, whether commanded or spontaneous, as political poets, in the broad sense of the word.

Before scientific history began, respectable authors thought nothing of making the confident assertion that the University of Cambridge was founded by Cantaber of Spain, 4,321 years after the Creation, or by King Arthur ; that the University of Oxford owed its origin to King Alfred ; and that the prime founder of the British Kingdom was a refugee from Troy. To a generation unfamiliar with documents, impatient of exact research, and fond (as all healthy people are) of the picturesque, there was nothing unnatural in the neat pedigrees of the Laureateship produced by the antiquaries of the seventeenth century. In Dryden's patent, " Sir Geoffrey Chaucer, Knight," " Sir John Gower, Knight," and " Benjamin Jonson, Esquire," were all specifically mentioned as having fully and amply enjoyed " the rights, privileges, benefits, and advantages thereunto belonging " in the time of " our Royall Progenitors." Where supposed experts were so dogmatic, it was not strange that laymen should take the antique lineage of the Laureateship on trust. These poets and others had received pensions and liquor from the Crown, and some of them were called poets

laureate. But the pensions—notably Chaucer's—
had not always any obvious connection with their
poetry ; the title was a mere degree given by the
Universities ; and there was no question of a regular
Post in the Household to which these men were
appointed. Their positions varied. Spenser received
money from Elizabeth, but his contact with her was
of the slenderest. Ben Jonson was pensioned over a
long period of years by two monarchs and supplied
many Court Masques in return for the favour. It
was not until the nomination of Dryden that the
Laureateship was recognised as a definite salaried
office which ought to be filled. Nevertheless, I feel
that Professor Broadus is a little rigid in his insistence on the fact. Most of our institutions have
shadowy beginnings, and the development of the
Laureateship may be regarded as analogous to that
of the Peerage, Parliament, and the Power of the
Purse. And at least I think we ought to shift the birth
of the regular office back to Davenant ; Davenant
may not have had a patent, but the fact that when
he died Dryden was in terms mentioned as his successor shows that he was already considered to be
holding an office, even if his status was only posthu-
mously recognised on paper.

After the date of Dryden's appointment, Professor Broadus distinguishes three clearly marked
epochs. Until the Georges came, the Laureates,
though any political writing they might do was
appreciated, were not expected to compose particular poems on particular dates. Dryden may have
been moved to write four great poems by virtue of
his official position, but he was not asked for New

Year Odes, and Tate, though prolific in these compositions, committed them voluntarily. It was with the appointment of Nicholas Rowe, in 1715, that the stated duties began. Until George III's time, the Laureate was compelled to furnish annually a New Year's Ode and a Birthday Ode, to be sung before the King by royal musicians in the Chapel Royal. Pope maliciously referred to Cibber's Odes as being

> made by the poet Laureate for the time being, to be sung at Court on every New Year's Day, the words of which are happily drowned by the instruments.

Whitehead, himself Laureate, wrote a very frank " Pathetic Apology for all Laureates," in which he said :

> His Muse, obliged by sack and pension
> Without a subject or invention,
> Must certain words in order set
> As innocent as a Gazette . . . .
> Content with Boyce's harmony,
> Who throws on many a worthless lay
> His music and his powers away.

He, a patient and a sensible man, sometimes managed to combine a humane and eloquent passage in an official poem, but more often produced verses which deserved his own candid description ; the only men who were probably comfortable with the job were the obscure Eusden and the worthless Pye. A typical passage is Colley Cibber's panegyric on the off-spring of George II :

> Around the royal table spread,
> See how the beauteous branches shine !
> Sprung from the fertile genial bed
> Of glorious GEORGE and CAROLINE.

The task was usually unpalatable ; one offer made in the middle of the century was coupled with an assurance that Odes would not be insisted upon. But the offer was declined, and the obligation continued until George IV released Southey, who had insisted when he was " inducted into all the rights, privileges and benefits which Henry James Pye, Esq., did enjoy," that he wished that " upon great public events I might either write or be silent as the spirit moved," and had only under protest supplied (not for publication) Odes for a few birthdays of the old mad blind George III.

Then began the third period. Since then the Laureate has been free " to write or be silent." Mr. Broadus rightly says that Tennyson was a national spokesman as no previous Laureate has been, and he calls attention to the fact, too often ignored, that during the late war the present Laureate produced a series of poems " of memorable quality and substantial length." " It is not," he says, " the ephemeral impulses of the war which find expression in Mr. Bridges' pages, but rather the greater emotions—the emotions which will still emerge as the perspective lengthens, and will sum up all the rest." " Throughout the war, and since the war was won,

Mr. Bridges has performed a service to which this history affords no parallel."

Is the Laureateship worth having ? Professor Broadus's book gives emphatic support to the view that " command " poems are, as a rule, likely to be bad. Even the ablest and most patriotic of genuine poets will probably produce a frigid and hollow-sounding composition if he be ordered to celebrate a nation, a hero, or a cause on a particular date. But this is not, as it has so often been supposed to be, sufficient ground for a condemnation of the Laureate-ship as an institution. Those who make it so are cherishing a misconception of the historical facts. It was always supposed that an official Laureate would occasionally derive inspiration from national history and political events ; and there is sense in the assumption that a man publicly called to the position of national poet will find his thoughts turning more often than they might, in other circumstances, turn to those themes, and might more often be moved to genuine poetical utterance concerning them. The disciplined Poet Laureate, the bard working to a schedule, is another matter ; and he has never existed in this country except during the one Hanoverian century. He appeared and disappeared with the powdered wig, and it is inconceivable that he should come again. A Laureateship without set duties is not, as is so generally assumed, an obsolete survival ; it is precisely the Laureate-ship which was originally established. One common error is evident here ; another lies in the equally frequent statement that appointments to the Laureateship have nearly always been bad.

## THE LAUREATES

They have not. Excepting in the eighteenth century they have usually been very good. We may, with Professor Broadus, rule out Chaucer, Skelton, and Jonson as not being in the true Laureate sequence: but the rest are a very creditable list. When Dryden was appointed there was one greater poet living, but even the most tolerant of restored Stuarts could scarcely have been expected to select John Milton, whose head, in 1660, had narrowly escaped being stuck upon Temple Bar to rot with those of the regicides. In 1688 there was nothing better available than Shadwell, who received the appointment, and whose work, after all, still in a manner lives. Nahum Tate, who followed shortly after, was certainly not a very eminent man, though he contributed one classic to the language, the carol, " While Shepherds Watched their Flocks by Night." But, in the political circumstances, nothing better could have been done. The Georgian era undeniably saw a slump both in poetry and in Laureates. Yet it is worth remarking that even in the worst age of official taste the Laureateship was offered to the greatest poet of that age. Gray refused. That he should wear the mantle just relinquished by Cibber was a little too much to ask ; and he was a recluse. His own account of his refusal was characteristic :

Though I very well know the bland, emollient, saponaceous qualities both of sack and silver, yet if any great man would say to me, " I make you rat-catcher to His Majesty, with a salary of £300 a year and two butts of the best Malaga ; and though it has been usual to catch a mouse or

two, for form's sake, in public once a year, yet to
you, sir, we shall not stand upon these things," I
cannot say I should jump at it ; nay, if they would
drop the very name of the office and call me Sine-
cure to the King's Majesty, I should still feel a
little awkward, and think everybody I saw smelt
a rat about me ; but I do not pretend to blame
anyone else that has not the same sensations ; for
my part I would rather be sergeant-trumpeter or
pinmaker to the palace. Nevertheless, I interest
myself a little in the history of it, and rather wish
somebody may accept it that will retrieve the
credit of the thing, if it be retrievable, or ever had
any credit.

Whitehead, who received the reversion, was hardly
great enough to " retrieve the credit of the thing,"
but there was no one much better in a time when
graceful small poets were common and great poets
not to be found. Warton, his successor, was also a
good—and an unexpected—choice, considering the
material available. When Pye died, in 1813, Sir
Walter Scott was offered the Laureateship and
declined it ; Southey, not a mean figure, however
poorly he may compare in our eyes with two poets
then writing, accepted it, and began the restoration
of credit. In the last eighty years there have been
four Laureates, of whom one was a statesman's
practical joke, and the other three were Wordsworth, Tennyson, and Robert Bridges. No doubt
many good nineteenth-century poets did not hold
the Laureateship. You cannot kill a Laureate a
year in order to prove your ability to choose his

successor ; if Tennyson was Poet Laureate, Browning
and Matthew Arnold could never be Poets Laureate,
since the office is held for life. This point is often
overlooked ; the truth is that as a rule the appointments have been made very well.

So why not go on making them ? It would be
pointless to exaggerate the advantages of the thing.
Let us say no more than that any contact between
the State and good literature is to be welcomed,
and that the Laureateship has led to the enrich-
ment of our literature by a few good poems. Yet we
need not even go so far as that to justify a con-
tinuance of the office. If no more could be said for
it than that it will generally, or even occasionally,
give an advertisement to a meritorious poet, and
that it is an ancient and innocuous part of our national
system, it would be worth preserving. So many old
things compel their own abolition by becoming
positive obstructions, abuses, and nuisances, that
we should feel especially tender about the old things
that do no harm.

Let the Laureateship remain ; and let the butt of
sack be restored. The student of Professor Broadus's
book will find that from the earliest days all our
Court poets and Poets Laureate were paid partly
in wine. He will also find, and he ought not to be
surprised to find, that when the grant of a butt of
wine was commuted for a small additional grant
of money, the change was made at the request of
the egregious Pye, at once the most avaricious, the
most abstemious, and the most illiterate of all those
who have worn the British laurel. In so doing he
cheated all his successors. For a thrifty government

conveniently forgot to pay them the £26 in lieu of
wine, pretending that the sum was included in the
£100 which had always been paid, and which continued to be paid. As Southey wrote pathetically to
Walter Scott :

> The butt of sack is now wickedly commuted
> to £26 ; which said sum, unlike the canary, is
> subject to income-tax, land-tax, and heaven knows
> what beside. The whole net income is little more
> or less than £90.

Scott replied :

> Is there no getting rid of that iniquitous *modus*,
> and requiring the butt in kind ? I would have
> you think of it ; I know no man so well entitled
> to Xeres sack as yourself, though many bards
> would make a better figure at drinking it. I should
> think that in due time a memorial might get some
> relief in this part of the appointment—it should
> be at least £100 wet and £100 dry. When you
> have carried your point of discarding the ode, and
> my point of getting the sack, you will be exactly
> in the position of Davy in the farce, who stipulates
> for more wages, less work, and the key of the
> ale-cellar.

Mr. Bridges at present receives £72 from the Lord
Chamberlain's department and £27 from the Lord
Steward's " in lieu of a butt of sack." In other words,
Pye's greed simply resulted in a reduction of salary.
Mr. Bridges is not primarily a bacchanalian poet,

but I cannot think that he would object if some member of Parliament, with a soul above trickery, the Statute of Limitations, and the Gaming Act, should begin agitating for the undoing of an ancient wrong, and the restoration of a still more ancient perquisite.

# LETTERS

TWO years ago Mr. George Saintsbury announced that his "Notes From a Cellar Book" would be his last book. The universal comment was that a man who was still capable of producing a little masterpiece like that had no right to stop. He has not stopped. Nature was not to be driven out for good, even with a corkscrew. Mr. Saintsbury has returned to normal. His latest enterprise, *A Letter Book*, might be described as consisting of notes on the National Cellar of Letters. He has the advantage here of being able to illustrate his disquisition on growths with samples which the reader may taste for himself ; exquisite as it was, his last work would have been still more so had a similar provision been possible for those who studied it.

There is a suggestion in the preface that Mr. Saintsbury regards his volume as a cairn or mausoleum celebrating a dead art. He is not alone in thinking the English Letter a fit subject for an epitaph. We cannot, of course, be quite sure that our age will not produce great letter-writers. We never know what is going on behind the scenes in any regard ; history is bound to produce surprises—as, for instance, Disraeli's letters to Queen Victoria. But we do know for a certainty that the composition of good letters is demonstrably less general than it was in the eighteenth century. In that century all one's friends would have been writing long and polished epistles ; in this century they certainly do not. Communications have improved. A man must go as far as China before we feel he is really cut off from us, and not likely to drop in at any moment ; and even there he will be getting from cables and newspapers far more information about wars, politics, books, pictures, the weather, the movements of the great, and all the other topics of Horace Walpole than we could ever compress into informative letters. It is disheartening to tell a man things he must know already ; we are not equal to merely re-writing the newspapers in our own whimsical, picturesque, idiosyncratic styles.

We are always rushing about ; so are our correspondents ; our letters approximate to telegrams containing merely essential demands, instructions, private news, and a casual sentence of cheer merely inserted to give them a faint touch of humanity. The Gray or the Cowper, living in some rustic vicarage or other such secluded retreat, may still be communicating, in leisurely style, with a few old friends about household affairs, eccentric literature, the migrations of swallows and the manners of ducks. If he is, so much the better for posterity ; but he will lack the background of lesser lights. In the great age almost every educated person wrote good letters; the existing stores are not yet fully explored. In our age we know from our own experience that this is not so. And I fancy that our posterity will be especially poorer by virtue of the lack of substantial letters from eminent writers, whose lives and private opinions arouse so natural a curiosity. Gray, Cowper, Lamb, Keats, Shelley, Byron, Browning—their letters, crowded with interest, fill many volumes. But I have never heard that any of our great

contemporaries has shown the slightest inclination to
such discursiveness ; the best literary letters that
I have seen have been tapped out on typewriters :
letters can be done so much more quickly on typewriters. Let us console ourselves with the reflection
that there are already far more fine English letters
in existence than most of us have managed to read ;
a man, before seriously complaining, should go
through the sixteen volumes of Horace Walpole.
Our letters are one of the glories of our literature,
and any book which calls attention to them should
be welcome.

Two good sorts of anthologies of letters may be
conceived. Mr. Lucas, in his delightful collections,
drew his materials from anywhere and everywhere.
He was in search of the most amusing and charming
things he could find ; he roped in every sort of
author ; his books exist for their own sakes. Mr.
Saintsbury's collection is of the other kind. With
the exception of a few engaging things such as that
by Ballard (of the " British Ladies ") his specimens
are entirely drawn from the letters of great letter-
writers and great authors—they include, by the way,
an unpublished example of Stevenson. They are
chosen avowedly to illustrate his historical sketch
of the progress of the art : the chief figures must all
be here, and no great amount of space can be allowed
to any of them : we have but one letter from Lamb,
but one from Cowper, but one from Walpole, but
two from Gray. They are freshly chosen, and a book
which contained nothing but these and the two noble
love-letters of Dorothy Osborne would be worth
reading. Scarcely anything in the book could be

superseded by anything better unless it be Ruskin's letter to the *Daily Telegraph*, chosen, I fear, with a touch of malice, which is full of nobility and wisdom, but is oh ! how far from being intimate ! But the volume is rather a chapter of history than an anthology. And, in fact, Mr. Saintsbury's own writing fills a half of it. His introduction is a hundred pages long : a masterly summary of the ways and means of correspondents from the earliest ages. In the course of it Mr. Saintsbury not merely sketches and explains the general changes which have taken place from age to age, but does full justice to all the great letter-writers in our language, amongst whom it is pleasant to notice that he puts Lady Mary Montagu, who, in our day, has received little lip-service, and scarcely any real attention. And the whole essay is, one need scarcely say, amusing and provocative in the extreme. So are the notes. Mr. Saintsbury's first extract comes from the letters of Synesius, who was Bishop of Ptolemais in the early fifth century. It begins :

I have already got three hundred spears and as many cutlasses, though I had, even before, only half a score two-edged swords : and these long flat blades are not forged with us. But I think the cutlasses can be struck more vigorously into the enemies' bodies, and so we shall use them. And at need we shall have bludgeons—for the wild olive trees are good with us.

Of the bludgeon referred to Mr. Saintsbury says in a footnote that " it was probably like the *lathi* which the mild Hindoo takes with him to political meetings." It is a characteristic start for Mr. Saintsbury, who himself has never attended the most academic of confabulations without his bludgeon. It was distressing a few years ago to see him formally abdicating this formidable weapon, as Prospero his wand ; and now all the more delightful to see him in the arena again clubbing right and left. His notes to the letters are full of his old gay pugnacity, with clean downright words for all the authors, critics, politicians, puritans, social institutions, and historical developments which he considers inimical to truth, good taste and the joy of life.

There never was a better writer of footnotes ; every sentence Mr. Saintsbury writes has his character stamped upon it, and his memory, which is as prodigious as his erudition, enables him to juxtapose the most surprising variety of illustrations. Independent judgments, odd facts, and comic stories appear on every page. Discussing whether or not Dorothy Osborne was born in the Castle in Guernsey, he says that " the present writer (who has danced, and played whist, within its walls) hopes she was." It isn't exactly evidence, but it is pleasant to know it. Encountering a denunciation, very justifiable, of lecturing by Charles Lamb, he puts as footnote :

Lamb would have enjoyed a recent newspaper paragraph, which, stating that an inquest had been held on someone who, after lecturing somewhere, was taken ill and expired, concluded thus : " Verdict : Death from natural causes."

He remarks of Ruskin that " If anybody ever could write beautifully about a broomstick ' he could : though perhaps it is a pity he so often did." A mention of a pike in Kingsley's racy letter to Tom Hughes gives him occasion for a dissertation on the pike's physiognomy : " And in fact the pike is not a cheerful-looking fish. Even two whom the present writer once saw tugging at the two ends of one dead trout in a shallow, did it sulkily." Introducing his selection from Charles Lamb, he recalls to mind " Mr. Matthew Arnold's very agreeable confession, when he was asked to select his poems, that he wanted to select them all." Mr. Saintsbury is, in fact, always and everywhere racy : as much of a piece as Charles Lamb himself : and if you can enjoy him at all, you can enjoy the whole of him. Had he written that unfortunately-abandoned " History of Wine," which he contemplated for so many years, it would have been as lively as his " History of the French Novel " ; in a Grammar or a Study of Fluctuations in Prices he would be as lively, as original, as anecdotal, as he is anywhere. Give him any excuse, and he will start pouring out quotations, allusions, challenges, dogmatic judgments, recollections, and jokes from his vast horn of plenty. The present volume is one more instalment of him ; and no assurances of his will prevent one from expecting more.

# GLANDS

THE book before me is entitled *The Glands Regulating Personality*, and its author is Dr. Louis Berman, of Columbia University. This is not the kind of book which I normally review, or have any scientific competence to discuss. But I took it up casually, and a phrase in it struck me. Dr. Berman remarks :

> To bring to mind an immediate complete image of the hyperthyroid face, one should think of Shelley.

This agreeable association of ideas led me on ; and finding the phrase, " A man's chief gift to his children is his internal secretion composition," I knew I must go through with it. Here, beyond doubt, was one more of these men with an explanation, satisfactory to himself, of everything that exists. So through thyroid and pituitary, pineal, adrenal and thymus I pursued my way, marvelling at one of the most remarkable medleys of erudition, illogicality, lack of taste, disinterested passion, complacency and bad English that I have seen since I read Freud's most humourless masterpiece, namely, his book on Wit.

Dr. Berman takes the glands one by one and outlines their spheres of influence. He compares them to the Directors of a Large Corporation : he might almost call them our Glandlords. From one to another he passes in an almost lyrical strain. For example : " In such enthusiasm for the thyroid as

246

a determinant of evolution, its pillar of cloud by day and column of fire by night, one should not forget the other glands of internal secretion." *En route* he throws out numerous definitions. " Masculinity," he says, "may be described as a stable, constant state in the organism of lime salts, and the feminine as an unstable variable state of lime salts." " The mother expresses," he observes, " the deep craving of protoplasm for immortality." And, in a phrase reminiscent of Sir William Harcourt's, " We are all Socialists now," he says that we now recognise that " we are all, more or less, partial hermaphrodites." Almost everything has been run down except the fluid of love, which, beyond doubt, exists in the interstitial cells. Having done with the separate glands, he passes to consider their influence on personality. He uses Mr. Strachey's account of Florence Nightingale for a ruthless analysis of the glands that made her what she was ; Cæsar, Napoleon, and Nietzsche are other of his specimens. He regrets that they did not live later, so that science could have rectified them. For the answer to " What is Man ? " has been found. It is—I don't think it a very complete answer—" Man is regulated by his glands of Internal Secretion."

" The chemistry of the soul ! " It is, says Dr. Berman, a great phrase. He looks forward—and, reading his book, one is tempted at times to share in this Larger Hope—to a time when statesmen will make it their business to raise the general level of intelligence by a " judicious use of endocrine extracts." " Internal glandular analysis may become legally compulsory for those about to mate before

the end of the present century." And then he becomes rhapsodic :

> The exact formula is yet far beyond our reach.
> But we have started upon the long journey and
> we shall get there. Then will Man truly become
> the experimental animal of the future, experi-
> menting not only with the external conditions of
> his life, but with the constituents of his very
> nature and soul. The chemical conditions of his
> being, including the internal secretions, are the
> steps of the ladder by which he will climb to those
> dizzy heights where he will stretch out his hands
> and find himself a God.

It is a strange idea of God. I suppose it doesn't
much matter. The man who wants to Get Omniscient
Quick is no new type. Pedantry, self-satisfaction,
fantastic exaggeration are as old as the race. One
would not even say, " Physician, inject thyself,"
to Dr. Berman ; such men as he add to the colour
of life ; they rode other hobby-horses in the days of
" Tristram Shandy," but their character, or glandular
composition, remains unchanged. It is, however, a
pity that they should now be commonest in the
world of what used to be called exact science ; for
the excesses of the Freudians and their analogues
have led many intelligent people into a very sceptical frame of mind about every scientific discovery
and speculation whatsoever, particularly when these
have a bearing upon the constitution of man. Twenty
years ago William James, meeting Freud, described
him in a letter as a monomaniac. The frontiers of

psychology and physiology are infested by hosts of these ill-balanced persons who get hold of a little truth and turn it into an idol. Dr. Berman himself has an excellent image for the Freudians : he says they look at a small section of life through a telescope and think it is the universe. The metaphor applies precisely to himself ; it is well enough, in a poet's sense, to see the universe in a grain of sand, but it is grotesque to see it in the glands. At best all he could do would be merely to identify a machine, and one amongst many.

He and his fellows may, however, win disciples amongst the large number of persons who are now able to dabble in this kind of easy science. And the one really serious result may be the infection of literature with it. I note such a passage as :

> Christina may be adrenal cortex centred and so masculinoid : courageous, sporty, mannish in her tastes, aggressive towards her companions. Dorothea may have a balanced thyroid and pituitary, and so lead the class as good-looking, studious, bright, serene, and mature. Florence, who has rather more thyroid than her pituitary can balance, will be bright but flighty, gay but moody, energetic, but not as persevering.

It may prove very tempting to our novelists. All over the fiction of Europe and America the Freudian complexes are raging furiously together ; when the novelists have tired of these they may get on to the glands ; we shall have the Tragedy of a Pineal and the conflict between two highly-developed

Adrenals. In one thing alone there is a gleam of hope.
There is less satisfaction for the morbid curiosity
in the glandular compilations than in the works of
Freud and his school ; less sensational material.
Nobody will take up with the glands out of a desire
to be audacious and shocking ; they are dull affairs.

I revert to the phrase with which I opened. I
cannot leave it there. One of my more highly-
developed glands is secreting hard. Here is the
result. A Ballade of the Glandular Hypothesis :

## I

What Hormones had that proud Egyptian Queen ?
  And great Napoleon, who had cause to rue
Deficiency of the central endocrine
  Which finally dried up at Waterloo ?
Poor Shelley's optimism was undue,
  He never should have dreamed at such a pace ;
He said " The world's great age begins anew " ;
  But Shelley had a hyper-thyroid face.

## II

There is a strange secretion flows between
  The interstitial cells ; I grant it's true
It hasn't yet been actually seen,
  Not even by the pioneering few ;
Still it will soon be bottled, and on view,
  The stuff that made an end of Ilium's race,
And launched a thousand ships into the blue :
  But Shelley had a hyper-thyroid face.

# GLANDS

## III

The toad secretes too much adrenalin,
    And drunkards are a thymo-centric crew,
Glandular hyper-functioning has been
    Noted in Florence Nightingale ; and you
Remember Mr. Julian Huxley drew
    Very strange transformations which took place
In certain axolotls in the Zoo :
    But Shelley had a hyper-thyroid face.

### ENVOI.

Prince, let us end our rhymes, they will not do :
    Our gonads may be large and full of grace,
And comely our pituitaries, too—
    But Shelley had a *hyper-thyroid* face.

# A SUPPLEMENT TO WHITMAN

PEOPLE used to say that Whitman was recognised everywhere except in his own country ; that he had been accepted as a peer by the English poets and as an influence by the French poets before the generality of Americans were willing to see him as anything more than a grubby old man who had lived near Philadelphia. There was some truth in the charge, and it is still evident, whenever an academic history comes out, that in the eyes of many Americans Whitman's defects still obscure his achievement. But once an American becomes a disciple he becomes a very enthusiastic disciple indeed. To Horace Traubel, Whitman was very much what Buddha might have been. So, also, to Professor Emery Holloway, who must have devoted years to the excavation of Whitman's forgotten contributions to newspapers, and whose tone, in his introduction, seems to suggest the conviction that any small fact about Whitman is of prime importance. There is certainly a good deal of information of all sorts in this introduction. We are told that much of the poet's early life " was to be spent in boarding-houses and hotels, a fact which doubtless had its influence in shaping his rather detached attitude towards the family as an institution " ; that his early Puritanism led him to " excoriate " the users of even tea, coffee, and tobacco ; and that when he first meditated a long book he proposed to omit all reference to sex, on the ground that he knew nothing whatever about it. Later on, *quantum mutatus !* But informative as the introduction is, I don't think that anybody could call it critical. And, indeed, if Professor Holloway were a critical admirer of Whitman, or, indeed, a critical lover of any literature whatsoever, he certainly would not have thought it worth while to resurrect the contents of these volumes, writings which Whitman himself had deliberately refrained from reprinting, and some of which are so feeble that it is difficult to remember that the author of them was a man of genius.

It would be complimentary to say even that the contents of these two volumes are worth having. Those who are interested in anything that Whitman did may like to see them once ; those who are merely interested in good literature will regard them as so much wasted paper. The poetry is remarkably little in proportion to the prose ; only thirty-one pages out of many hundreds, with the addition of a few pages of scraps from notebooks. Such as it is, it shows that Whitman, before casting off the " bondage " of rhyme, attempted with very small success to write poetry both in manner and in matter resembling the conventional verses of his time. Take the " Spanish Lady," which begins :

> On a low couch reclining
>     When slowly waned the day,
> Wrapt in gentle slumber,
>     A Spanish maiden lay.
>
> O beauteous was the lady ;
>     And the splendour of the place
> Matched well her form so graceful,
>     And her sweet, angelic face.

But what doth she so lonely,
    Who ought in courts to reign ?
For the form that there lies sleeping
    Owns the proudest name in Spain.

'Tis the lovely Lady Inez,
    De Castro's daughter fair,
Who in the castle chamber
    Slumbers so sweetly there.

This, in point both of metrical distinction and content, is about on a par with

    Little drops of water,
    Little grains of sand.

Whitman wrote it at the age of twenty-one. But he was twenty-seven when he produced the " Ode to be sung at Fort Greene," beginning :

O God of Columbia ! O Shield of the Free !
    More grateful to you than the fanes of old story,
Must the blood-bedewed soil, the red battleground,
    be
    Where our forefathers championed America's
    glory !
Then how priceless the worth of the sanctified earth
We are standing on now. Lo ! the slopes of its girth
    Where the martyrs were buried : Nor prayers,
    tears, or stones,
    Marked their crumbled-in coffins, their white
    holy bones.

At twenty-nine he was producing blank verse a long way after Wordsworth's. At thirty he was feeling his way with free verse ; but this collection contains only two or three scraps of verse from the later period, none of them worth having except as " documents."

Prose fills up the greater part of these volumes ; but Whitman's " uncollected " prose is not much more interesting than his " uncollected verse." The first prose piece quoted is dated 1838. It is taken from the " Long Island Democrat," and is described as " the earliest extant prose from Whitman's pen." I think I had better quote it in full in order to illustrate what happens when enthusiasts get hold of a modern writer. It is headed "Effects of Lightning" —as it might be " Strange Happening on an Omnibus " or " Woman Faints at Princess Mary's Wedding "—and this is how it goes :

At Northport, on Sunday, 28th ultimo, an unfortunate and somewhat singular accident occurred from the lightning. Mr. Abraham Miller, of that place, had been in the fields engaged in some farm work, and was returning home, as a storm commenced in the afternoon, carrying in his hands a pitchfork. A friend of his, who was with him, advised him not to carry it, as he considered it dangerous. Mr. Miller, however, did not put down the fork, but continued walking with it ; he had gone some distance home, and had just put up the bars of a fence he passed through, when a violent clap of thunder occurred, followed by a sharp flash. The acquaintance of Mr. Miller was slightly stunned by the shock, and, turning round to look at his companion, he saw him lying on his face motionless. He went to him and found him dead, the lightning, having been attracted by the steel tines of the fork, had torn his hand slightly and killed him on the instant.

We may be exceedingly sorry for Mr. Abraham Miller without thinking that the tale of his demise was worth printing ; a single line to the effect that Whitman was " at this time engaged in journalism" would have sufficed as a substitute. The later papers are better than this. There are fragments of fiction ; there are essays ; there are obituaries ; there are political tracts ; there are fragments of literary criticism. Some of these last have a certain interest. The young Whitman boldly defended Dickens against those who accused the novelist of painting horrible pictures of low life. The poor, he said, were shown examples of worth by poverty deprest, and the rich were made to taste " distresses of want " which were beyond their immediate experience. He said, stupidly, of Dr. Johnson that " he was a sour, malicious, egotistical man " and " a sycophant of power and rank " ; that his heart could only be indicated by " the sign minus," and that " his soul was a bad one." William Cullen Bryant he described as " one of the best poets in the world " ; he liked Carlyle ; he said that

> Keats—peace to his ashes—was one of the pleasantest modern poets, and, had not the grim monster, Death, so early claimed him, would doubtless have become one of the most distinguished.

# A SUPPLEMENT TO WHITMAN

He called Lamb " the pleasant Elia," he argued that less than justice was done to Longfellow, " an honour and a glory as he is to the American name," and an equal of Wordsworth ; he described Melville as " readable," and he was extremely enthusiastic about authors as varied as Ruskin, James Thomson, and Martin Tupper, whom he described as " one of the rare men of the time." A large portion of the second volume is occupied by a novel, written in the interests of Temperance, alias total abstinence. It is headed :

FRANKLIN EVANS,
or
THE INEBRIATE.
A Tale of the Times.

By WALTER WHITMAN.

and it was announced in the " New World " as being by " one of the best Novelists of this country " ; which was very misleading. The papers on the antiquities of Brooklyn, which conclude this collection, are, on the whole, much the most interesting—as they are almost the latest—of the pieces now brought together.

Whitman was never very successful in prose, though some of his table-talk is stimulating and amusing. We had better get back to " Leaves of Grass," his real legacy. That collection is at once an achievement, a revelation, and a warning. It contains some of the noblest poetry of modern times ; it also contains some of the flattest. Whitman was born a poet, but there were strains in his character which prevented him from making the most of his natural endowment. He had a multiplicity of objects ; he wished to Americanise America and to reform society in accordance with a programme of his own. He was extremely anxious to exhibit himself as the most free and independent citizen alive. He was anxious, especially after he found that traditional forms very much cramped his style, to liberate verse from the " shackles " of rhyme and regular rhythm with which an effete, aristocratic, and militarist Europe had invested it. The result was a great deal of " verse " which was no more than free prose, and pamphleteering or merely informative prose at that. There are included amongst his works very many poems, or parts of poems, like this :

I am the train.
Panting, rolling, roaring through tunnels,
Rattling along causeways, shrieking through flying towns,
I go from East to West, through Virginia, Kentucky, Missouri, Kansas, Arizona, to California.
I link East to West of this great Continent,
The pale clerk of the cities
And the bronzed red-shirted broncho-buster of the ranches.

Whitman did not write that : I have just done it myself. But Whitman might quite well have written it when uninspired : it ought not to be printed as anything but prose, and even as prose it is not good. He is often matter-of-fact, and, when not matter-of-fact, often rhetorical. And the important thing to note about him is that when he is at his best there is never any doubt that it is free verse he is writing and not free prose. Sometimes, as in " O Captain, my Captain," he is even impelled to make rhymes, though not very good ones ; always, as he rises to poetry, he tends to write like other poets, in rhythms more repetitive than those of prose. The anthologists drawing on him always draw on the same small group of poems : " When Lilacs First in the Door-yard Bloomed," " The Dirge for Two Veterans," and so on. In those poems, his best, he was least peculiar, more near to his brothers. He remained, usually, " free " ; he abstained from rhyme, and his lines, typographically, were of vary-ing lengths. So were Ossian's, Southey's, Blake's sometimes, Matthew Arnold's sometimes ; there was nothing novel in it. Being a genuine poet he did find his imagination stirred by certain things which had not previously been " mentioned " by poets ; but his deliberate cultivation of originality led to nothing at all.

# THE ELEMENTS OF POETRY

DURING the last ten years the appearance of a large and voluble school of writers who openly proclaim themselves to be in revolt against " conventional poetry " has led to a great deal of discussion in America as to the nature and development of the art. I suspect that the discussion is dying down ; I think that the extremer manifestations of " revolt " are waning, and that where the apostles of revolt are poseurs or fools they are being found out. But if a justification is to be found for all the bad " free verse " that has been written in America, and all the nonsense that has been talked about it, it is to be found in this book. Had the nonsense not been written, and had it not been taken seriously, Professor Lowes would not have found it desirable to re-examine the foundations of poetry. And had Professor Lowes not written *Convention and Revolt in Poetry* we should have forgone the best book about poetry which has been written in our generation. Those who have a wide acquaintance with books about literature written by American professors may rub their eyes at this statement. But it is true.

I know no book where so much of the ground is covered, no book in which so many true and valuable things about poetry, both " original " and " quoted," are contained. Professor Lowes goes considerably farther than his title might suggest. He found, immediately he approached the subject, that he could not argue the question for the benefit

of puzzled contemporaries without going back
to the very roots of the subject. He had to decide
what he meant by poetry (concluding, inevitably,
that he meant what all interested persons have
always meant), and he then had to examine, scientifi-
cally and historically, the common marks of poetry
in point of content, of form, and of diction. He notes
the universality, in poetry, of poetical rhythm, and
hints (he might have gone farther) at its basis.
He explains the " inevitability of imagery " on the
ground of the inadequacy of words—he might here
have noted the common association between unusual emotion and the use of imagery. He explains
how it is that, men being what they are, certain
" subjects " invariably recur in poetry. He shows
how the changing circumstances of each age modify
the treatment of those subjects and the language
and imagery employed. And he gives illustrations
of the recurrent phenomena of a hardening of convention and an excess of reaction against convention;
each of which leads to lying, musical deficiency,
and a diminution of poetic influence. So wide is his
range, and so fertile is he in suggestion, that it is
utterly impossible here to give even a synopsis of
his conclusions.

Professor Lowes concludes that " when dead
conventions squeak and gibber in the streets there
are just three ways of reckoning with them " :

Poets may set the conventions going with the
detachment of a phonograph, and even absent
themselves, to all intents and purposes, entirely.
Or they may exercise creative energy, as we have

seen, upon dead forms and empty shells, and bring about a metamorphosis. Or, finally, they may rise up in revolt, repudiate the old coinage altogether, and more or less definitely set themselves to minting new.

It doesn't much matter what happens, he says ; the wheel always returns. That is pessimistic. If reaction goes too far ; if it goes so far as to lead people away from poetry altogether ; if they altogether refuse to notice what they feel (for example) about love or death, and if they resist the rhythm when it comes, a generation's powers may be wasted. But Professor Lowes does not really leave us in doubt as to his position. He knows that "the history of English poetry is an illuminating record of periodical farewells to folly," and if the folly could be avoided and the second, and only fruitful one, of his courses be always pursued, he would be completely happy.

Only in one small particular do I find Professor Lowes's book defective. His principles are sound, but, in view of the fact that his disquisition was provoked by the widespread existence of " revolt " in his own country, he might have taken more pains to apply them to the contemporary. Except for one poem of Rupert Brooke's, and one not very admirable piece of free verse, he quotes nothing from modern English poets : in so far as he gives modern instances, his examples are drawn from American writers, and mostly from those who may ambiguously be called the Revolting School. His quotations are all pertinent, but he seems to suggest by implication that the sillier forms of revolt have been as conspicuous in England as in America. It is not so ; in so far as we have witnessed an outbreak here it has been an imported, but not an important, thing ; taken part in by persons whose affiliations are with America and Paris, and provoking very little serious discussion. If one age in our poetry has succeeded another the transition this time has been made with unusual ease. Our poets have incorporated new experiences, new words and new rhythms in the last twenty years ; they exhibit a surprising variety ; but the best of them, those with the greatest power of communicating thought and emotion and with the most evident gifts of craftsmanship, are as traditional as they are modern. The difference between the circumstances of the two countries may be illustrated by the fact that in America Mr. Robert Frost is regarded as a rebellious innovator, whereas here we regard him as thoroughly traditional. Convention, in the last generation, was, it appears, much harder in America than it was here, artificiality and prettiness and pedantry much more general ; the consequence being that a sincere and straightforward poet whose lines are not all drawn with a footrule is regarded as a portent, and that writers with less brain and heart than Mr. Frost are thrown into a state of excessive reaction against everything that has been done before. Professor Lowes should not suppose that anything analogous to what has been happening in America has been happening here ; we have had, as it were, a Mormon Mission, but nobody has taken any notice of it. Moreover, I think that if he compels himself to face facts, he will come to the conclusion that he himself does not really think very much of some of the " free verse " which he quotes. He is fairly cautious about it. He does seem to suggest that he doesn't see very much in it, but that it has been passed on to him as the representative work of its day, and that consequently he supposes it must be good. He goes so far in one place as to quote passages from the prose of Mr. Conrad, Walter Pater, and Mr. Hewlett, and set them against various so-called poems by young apostles of revolt. Here, arranged in the familiar typographical way, is a fragment from one of Mr. Conrad's novels :

> The bright domes
> Of the parasols
> Swayed lightly outwards
> Like full-blown blossoms
> On the rim of a vase. . . .
>
> The wheels turned solemnly ;
> One after another the sunshades drooped,
> Folding their colours
> Like gorgeous flowers shutting their petals
> At the end of the day.

And here is his extract from Mr. Hewlett :

> As he had seen her,
> So he painted. . . .
> A grey, translucent sea
> Laps silently
> Upon a little creek
> And, in the hush of a still dawn,
> The myrtles and sedges on the water's brim
> Are quiet. . . .

She would vanish, we know,
Into the daffodils
Or a bank of violets.
And you might tell her presence there,
Or in the rustle of the myrtles,
Or coo of doves
Mating in the pines ;
You might feel her genius
In the scent of the earth
Or the kiss of the West wind ;
But you could only see her
In mid-April,
And you should look for her
Over the sea.

Professor Lowes contrasts these with certain modern pieces of free verse. He does suggest that he cannot tell the difference between one and the other ; he is aware that there is a borderland between prose and verse, which both may be haunting ; it does not occur to him that in almost every instance his example from so-called prose is not merely more regularly rhythmical than his examples from so-called verse, but that it is usually, in point of intelligence and feeling, actually far better. Here, from one who is distinctly one of the most acute, economical, and painstaking members of the Revolt, is an image :

Sand cuts your petal,
Furrows it with hard edge,
Like flint
On a bright stone.

I am not quite sure what it means ; it might convey something to a Japanese. It moves me through none of my senses ; I do not know why it should be called verse, even free verse ; and my only answer is, " Well, what about it ? " I should not dream of suggesting that unrhymed verse written in irregular lines is necessarily inferior to rhymed verse in regular rhymes ; Arnold, Henley, and many before them, had written it. As I have already pointed out, it is noticeable that Whitman is most nearly traditional in point of rhythm when he is at his best, just as it is noticeable that Donne is least Donnishly crabbed and obscure when he is at his best : the finest achievements of the unorthodox are orthodox.

There is, Professor Lowes admits, some apparent physical connection between a high state of emotion and regularity of movement, and whenever prose-writers become exalted in feeling, they tend to be more regular in their rhythms. Grant that (and it is a matter beyond our control, however unreasonable we may presume to think it) and the utmost freedom is permissible if a man can make use of it. Most poets do, in point of fact, find it pleasant and salutary to add other forms of repetitiveness to the one that appears essential ; but if a man care to abandon rhyme, and even line, let him, especially if he finds that they cramp him. It may be significant that the positive achievements of the propagandist school of free-verse writers are almost negligible ; but a man should use whatever form suits him best. What is wrong with most of the free-verse writers is not that they write free-verse, but that they lack the qualities which make good poets in whatever form they may write. The worst of them are principally governed by a desire to attract attention or a desire to be different from other people, or a mere radical reaction against the established thing—which, for such are the conditions of life, is often the inevitable and necessary thing. The best of them are in some instances honest and intelligent, but devoid of passion and of ear, unacquainted with the emotions that have always produced what men have agreed to call poetry, or else so deluded by doctrine that they have failed to make a connection between the emotions they experience and the art they practise. It is not even enough to " keep the eye on the object " if there is nothing behind the eye.

# THE PROSPECTS OF ENGLISH

" THERE is," says Professor Matthews, at the opening of his *Essays on English*, " no topic about which men dispute more frequently, more bitterly, or more ignorantly, than about the right and the wrong use of words. . . . To misuse words, to make grammatical blunders, is an evidence of illiteracy ; and to accuse a man of illiteracy is to disparage the social standing of his father and his mother." He manages to avoid acerbity himself, and I hope that I shall keep my own black passions in control while writing this review.

It is a slight book, a series of papers, which not only avoid pedantry, but do not aim at any display of scholarship. The book is readable and uniformly sensible—a book intended for the non-specialist, which presents him with no difficulties. It is not a treatise, but a volume of good and useful journalism. Professor Matthews was apparently incited by finding that many of his colleagues in the American Academy were alarmed at the prospects of our tongue. They thought that degeneration had already begun, degeneration like that which marked the later history of Greek. This, they maintained, is our Hellenistic era. Professor Matthews, instinctively revolting against so dreary a view, set about an examination of the situation, and has now formulated his own opinion.

I assume that all, or almost all, of the readers of these lines will desire two things : that the English of England and America should retain both its vigour and its homogeneity, and that, if possible, its use should spread amongst the peoples of the world. Professor Brander Matthews, who speaks English himself, has inherited our modes of thought and feeling, and consequently desires the perpetuation and extension of Anglo-American civilisation, treats both these aspects of his subject. With regard to the latter, there is not much said and there is little to say. Political events in the end will probably determine the status of our language in the world. If we and the Americans retain the power we have we may look forward to a steady increase in the number of people to whom our tongue is a birthright, and we may reasonably hope that it (with French as its nearest competitor) will become the *lingua franca* of the world, with consequent results in the laws, manners, and morals of the world—for, honestly, the Germans are not the only people who have desired to disseminate their Kultur, though they made the ghastly mistake of thinking it possible to spread it by mere boasting and force of arms. Professor Matthews dismisses Volapuk (which is dead anyhow) and Esperanto ; has a kind word for Ido, and a kinder for Latin ; and concludes that French will ultimately share with English the privilege of being, amongst educated men, universal. Beyond that he does not go ; and, after all, prophecy here has gone far enough, As to the future of English (domestically), he is optimistic. I think that had he known more of current English he would have been more optimistic still.

The English language is in the charge of two great aggregations of states : the British Empire and the

Amèrican Union. It runs, or it may conceivably not run, two risks. On the one hand it may be muddied by too great an influx of new terms, flooding in from every quarter of the English-speaking globe ; on the other hand it may be the victim of fissiparous tendencies such as produced the divergence between Spanish and Portuguese. The first danger, Professor Matthews believes, is found on examination not to be serious. We are not taking words faster than our fathers did ; many are called but few are chosen ; colloquialisms change, but standard English remains, and it develops slowly. Its risks are rather of the other kind. There has been observable too rigid a reluctance to admit desirable terms from the popular speech, a slightly exaggerated inclination to Latinity. And, as Mr. Bridges has vigorously argued, our difficulty with regard to foreign importations is that we do not naturalise them as freely as our ancestors did ; we still write " ennui " and " nuance," and write them in italics. The words we get from the populace, at home and abroad, seldom stay unless they are really good and valuable. There is apparently little fear that English, as we speak it here, will merely run to seed so long as we do not. But is the unity of the English language threatened ? Is there any tendency on the part of English speech and American speech to diverge ?

The answer, I believe, is so obvious that it would not be worth making were it not that there are people in both countries who casually assume such a process to be inevitable. There are local differences, both of pronunciation and of vocabulary. But the popular speech of Illinois is no farther apart from that of Devonshire than that of Devonshire is from that of Whitechapel, and an educated American talks more like an educated Englishman than does an educated Scot who has remained at home. This is the fact ; since it is so after generations during which communications between the two continents were not so easy and frequent as they are now, and popular education was less widespread and uniform, there is ground for Professor Matthews's argument that, if anything, the future tendency of the two divisions of one speech will be to come closer. In these days even slang, provided it be really vivid slang, crosses the Atlantic very rapidly, and an American neologism which really meets a demand for a new word spreads to England instead of remaining a local, differentiating Americanism. " The self-governing dominions of the British Commonwealth," says Professor Matthews, " and the semi-independent states of the American Union are all of them proving-ground for verbal seedlings which may in time be transplanted and acclimated (we should say acclimatised) in standard English." Our acquisitions from America are varied. Amongst the earliest were Indian words such as " wigwam " and " totem." Many of the later ones have been double words, mostly metaphorical. Amongst them are " scare - head," " wind - jammer," " side - track," " side-step," " pussy-foot," " high-brow," " joy-ride," " spell - binder," " sky - scraper," " strap-hanger " (there never was a word we more acutely needed than that one), " rough-rider," " sky-pilot," " fool-proof," " gun-shy," " sky-light." " Boss " and " boom " are older than most of these. The first came out of New York, and the second from the lumber-camps of Michigan. There was a time when they were regarded here as Americanisms ; their origin is hardly realised now by most of those who habitually use them. Simultaneously new English coinages make their way into the United States. " Cad " and " fad " were at first only localisms ; they were Briticisms struggling for existence, and getting slowly into sporadic use in England, until at last they achieved a peaceful penetration into the United States. " Rough " has gone to America, " tough " may finally settle here. Some words and locutions do not seem to thrive overseas, but, if purely ephemeral slang be ruled out, they are not very numerous.

They are even less numerous than Professor Matthews thinks. He might have made his case stronger, but, like many Americans who write on the language, he is imperfectly acquainted with British practice ; he ought to have asked an Englishman to check his illustrations of divergence. He is perfectly correct in saying that the American " back of " has never won favour here, and that it probably never will ; he notes a " British localism " that may not spread in " directly," for " as soon as." But several words which he thinks we do not use we, as a fact, use daily. He is right—it is the first thing the Englishman is breathlessly told when he lands on the Island of Manhattan—in saying that what is a " tuxedo " in America is known only as a " dinner-jacket " in England. It is also true that a " drummer " is in England a " commercial traveller." But his authorities have misled him when they gave him to suppose that the word "bedspread" is unknown in England. He gives "cowboy" and "cuspidor" as words which have no British equivalent; we use the former to describe an object we do not ourselves produce, and our equivalent for the latter is the robust word, "spittoon." "Fall," for "autumn," though a good old English word, is no longer used in England ; but it is astonishing that Professor Matthews should believe that nobody in England uses the word "rooster," for "cock," or "wilt," for "wither." The word "rooster," he says, "has completely faded from memory in England." "There would," he proceeds,

> be advantage in explaining to the American visitor that, if he goes to an English hotel for a dinner at a fixed price, he will be at liberty to call for a second helping of anything which may please his palate if the bill-of-fare declares that "a follow of any dish will be served without extra charge."

But on what bill-of-fare is the word "follow" to be found, used as an equivalent for a second helping ? You may find the word in Dickens ; it may still be currently employed by the "plump headwaiter at the Cock " ; but where else can it be encountered ? Professor Matthews may be assured that the conventional English term—unless you happen to prefer "another go," "another whack," or, more quietly, "some more "—is precisely the same as the American. His conclusion stands : "We cannot help seeing that the divergencies between British English and American English are relatively very few if only we keep in mind the immense vocabulary of our ever-expanding language."

Many other aspects of language development are touched on by Professor Matthews. He has a good deal to say about the coinage of new words. One is astonished when one reflects how rapidly it is proceeding. The new words swarm ; words of all kinds ; " dope," " enthuse," " peeved," " addict," " secretariat," " personnel," " opt," " national " (the noun)—they are everywhere, and we may devoutly hope that not all of them will surivive, for not all of them are needed. Professor Matthews calls attention to the influence of headline-writers—who must have short words—on the language. He remarks on the degeneration of words : somebody once said that no modern writer would dare to say that " Adam led his blooming Eve out of her blasted Paradise." He has some interesting pages about words which have come back into currency after having been long regarded as archaic, these including such familiar vocables as " anthem," " deluge," " problem," " illusion," " sphere," " phantom," " plumage," and " shapely." He deprecates the use of words in writing which we find it impossible to use in speech, giving " irrefragable " as an example ; elsewhere I notice himself using that signal specimen " inexpugnable." And he argues very strongly in favour of the complete naturalisation, phonetically and typographically, of foreign words which we have decided that we cannot do without. There is an unanswerable case in favour of this. It is grotesque to go on writing *rôle* and *mêlée* as we do ; our ancestors would have standardised

" shover " and " garridge " by now. An elaboration of that argument may be found in one of the early tracts of the Society of Pure English. The latest tract issued by this deserving Society deals with something less vital, but very interesting. It registers some of the French borrowings from English, demonstrating that our exports are substantial as well as our imports. Until the late seventeenth century the French took virtually nothing from us ; but since the Huguenots began translating English books into French the process of absorption has never flagged. The English vocabularies of war, millinery and cookery are almost wholly derived from France ; but the French have drawn quite as freely on us for their vocabularies of sport and politics.

# DELICATE DETAILS

EVERY day, and in every way, we are learning more and more about Swinburne's life at Putney. Man after man who had luncheon at " The Pines " has described the meal ; many new facts came to light in the recent " Life of Watts-Dunton " ; and now Mrs. Watts-Dunton comes along with a mass of new information which she was in a peculiar position to obtain. She had, says the publisher of the *Home Life of Swinburne,* " exceptional opportunities for studying the great poet in the various phases of his everyday life. No one living had the close association with him which she enjoyed as the wife of Swinburne's dearest and closest friend, and no one else could have drawn this faithful picture, full of delicate details, of the last years of his life." From early girlhood Mrs. Watts-Dunton had been accustomed to revere Swinburne. She had at school a Canadian governess who would " declaim at odd moments, in a voice throbbing with a sense of their beauty, that soul-stirring lyric which begins : ' When the hounds of spring are on winter's traces.' " The governess often had " Laus Veneris " with her when the girls were playing tennis, and " when it was time to return to the house she would cause me to walk beside her, and then I would hear about ' Anactoria ' and the other glorious pieces to be found within the covers of her cherished volume." Judge, then, the young girl's excitement when she was first asked to dinner, found Watts " waiting to receive me in his charming dining-room which, contrary to a published account, is not connected by folding doors with the adjoining room," and was taken out into the garden and asked " to partake of the biggest, fattest gooseberries I had ever seen." Judge, again, her delight when she met Swinburne, and,

> looking hard at me out of those wonderful eyes, he ejaculated two or three times the word "*Tiens!*"

And imagine with what a keen observation, when she went to " The Pines " as a wife, she noted everything which was likely to interest future students of the poet's works.

It is impossible to do more than give an idea of the wealth of the material which she now makes available. Here, as she says, is something " apropos de bottes." " A brilliant essayist wrote in a leading review " that Swinburne had small hands and feet. He had not :

> I had ample opportunity for knowing a good deal about the footwear of the Housemates. The same boot-maker made for both of them. There was but little difference in size, Swinburne's feet being a trifle larger than Walter's. The poet took what, in the trade, is called " an eight and a half," so that to write of his " tiny feet " is absurd. Swinburne had his boots made of calf leather, while Walter preferred a soft kid. Often when I was out walking with Walter I would notice that he had on a pair of calf boots. I would say, " You've got Swinburne's boots on again. Oh, dear ! Why will you not look ? "

Swinburne did not wear his hair long ; " the little he possessed was often cut by the barber." He had a horror of drawing small cheques. " Lord Burnham may be interested to learn that Swinburne's morning paper was the *Daily Telegraph*." He was fond of Christmas and often bought presents for his friends :

He always seemed quite pleased with everything he had bought, yet he appeared uncertain as to what the recipient would think of the little gifts. He would inquire anxiously, " Do you think he " (or " she," as the case might be) " will like it ? " On being reassured on this head, he would give a little satisfied sigh, as if the question were quite momentous, and murmur with relief, " Oh, I'm so glad you think so too ! "

It is untrue that he was always moving his arms and legs about. " He made," says Mrs. Watts-Dunton, " no convulsive movement in the intimacy of our domestic circle," and it can only be presumed that " the strangers who took note of his spasmodic movements . . . were themselves the cause of the ' symptom ' they deplored." Swinburne swore when annoyed, and " I fear it may come as a shock to the æsthetic devotees of Swinburne to learn that the hideous word, ' bloke,' was not foreign to his vocabulary. Coming from him it sounded dreadful."

" Here in this room," says Mrs. Watts-Dunton, recollections drive on me in waves ; my memory is suddenly like a stream in spate. And the difficulty with me is what to select as memorable and what to reject as trivial."

# DELICATE DETAILS

Her gift of selection proves to be almost infallible, and she leaves our knowledge of Swinburne's character, habits, and tastes considerably extended. There are, however, some things which remain to be cleared up ; there are a few bewildering problems which still call for solution if we are to have that complete biographical insight which is necessary to a full understanding of "Atalanta" and "Tristram of Lyonesse." The size of Swinburne's feet is now ascertained once and for all, and it will be impossible for any future critic, however revolutionary, to reopen the question of the kind of soap which he used in his bath. Much is established ; but much remains to be established. " The Art of biography," a poet has written,

> Is different from geography ;
> Geography is about Maps,
> But Biography is about Chaps.

Nevertheless, it is impossible not to see a resemblance between the progress of the two arts : not to think, when such works as Mrs. Watts-Dunton's are published, of the piecemeal amplification of knowledge through the local surveys of successive explorers : not to visualise the life of a great dead man as a continent which is gradually surveyed. In the map of Swinburne there are still several blank spaces which remain to be filled up. His biographers have thus far been completely silent about certain aspects of his diet. We know from Mrs. Watts-Dunton the development of his tastes in drinks, the sort of tumbler he fancied, the pleasure he took in partridge-pie, and his attitude towards shell-fish. This last is illustrated in a passage so full and final that I feel compelled to quote it :

> Here, as illustrating a self-control with which he is seldom credited, I record his avoidance of those dishes which he knew from experience were not good for him. For instance, he avoided shell-fish, although he liked it. Lobster or crab was never served. I remember once buying some aspic jelly which I made into moulds with very pink shrimps showing through the gelatinous transparency. He was immensely pleased with the appearance of the dainty. "How very pretty those little things look—almost too pretty to eat !" was his comment. "But I think I *must* this time because *you* prepared it."

It is a heartening episode ; our mediæval ancestors would have made of it a Morality Play in which the issue should lie between four characters, Courtesy and Dyspepsia on the one side and Churlishness and Good Digestion on the other, the conflict between Appetite and Medical Advice being the theme for a subsidiary plot. Lobster was banished from Swinburne's life, shrimps admitted only occasionally, and with a gallant gesture ; but what of early morning tea ? It is a fairly full account of Swinburne's normal day that Mrs. Watts-Dunton gives us, but, following for once the usual custom of biographers in omitting the things which interest us most, she is silent regarding the very beginning of his mornings. Did he or did he not take tea in bed ? If he did was it his habit to take it (*a*) alone, (*b*) with bread and butter, or (*c*) with biscuits ? With regard to clothes, again, there are important points to be cleared up. He invariably, we now know, wore soft collars and shirts, and liked them clean ; he refused to be measured for his clothes ; and his boots were of calf and of an eight-and-a-half size.

But there is a question still outstanding. Some people might hesitate to ask it, even in an age when we have grown accustomed to the most brutal frankness about the most intimate and sacred details of private life. But I find it impossible not to express my curiosity about it : Did Swinburne wear sock suspenders ? So very much hangs upon them. We have already certain data which would give future critics a basis for speculation, even were no further information forthcoming from authoritative sources. But the data conflict, and if no more are supplied the Problem is likely to be as endlessly fruitful of controversy as is that of the identity of Shakespeare's " Mr. W. H." On the one hand Swinburne's passion for neatness, and especially sartorial neatness, is clear. But on the other hand we have his equally evident inability to understand or employ the complex mechanical devices of this inventive age. He was amazed at the marvels of photography. The thought of teaching him to use a typewriter was no sooner entertained than abandoned. He was delighted with a present of an eighteen-penny napkin-ring, for " I doubt if Swinburne had ever heard of celluloid." Further :

His intelligence was so confined to pretty and imaginative literature that even the mechanism of a soda-water syphon was beyond him. When for the first time I manipulated one in his presence, he gazed at me, evincing considerable apprehension for my safety. I succeeded in releasing a gentle stream into my glass. When I stopped, he said with an accent of admiration and surprise, "How cleverly you did that; I couldn't have done it." I could disclaim the compliment, but I could not truthfully contradict the second part of his comment.

On the whole, in the light of this, I incline to think that Swinburne's socks must have been left to struggle with the force of gravity unassisted by mechanical aids ; but if Mrs. Watts-Dunton can clear the matter up in a supplement to this book, all lovers of literature will be grateful. And another point is : did none of his modernistic friends introduce him to the mystery of bath salts ? " Next to love of his friends came Swinburne's love of the sea. And next to his love of the sea ranked his love of babies." His friends and babies he could see at Putney ; but Putney has no more sea-coast than Bohemia. Salt and ozone being essential, Swinburne was happy in discovering a brand of soap called Samphire Soap :

This precious tablet smelt of the sea, or was supposed to smell of the sea. A. C. S. believed implicitly that it was highly charged with the active principle of ozone. He sensed the wave in its odour, and the suds in his bath were refreshing to him as the foam of the ocean. Needless to say, " Samphire " soap was a thing of which we never permitted ourselves to " run short."

" I still," adds Mrs. Watts-Dunton, " keep a cake of it as a souvenir of the happiest time of my life." The time is probably not far off when it will be generally felt that so precious a relic as a cake of Swinburne's Soap ought not to remain indefinitely in private hands. But there a larger question is opened up. Is it not time that steps should be taken to ensure the future of " The Pines " ? Ought not a Swinburne Memorial Committee to be established with a view of acquiring it, if and when it comes into the market, as a permanent home for the soap, and other relics ? These are difficult times, and people have little money to spare ; but surely we have here an exceptional case.

I cannot conclude this all too summary review of a fascinating volume without a wish that other great poets had been so fortunate in their biographers as Swinburne has been in Mrs. Watts-Dunton. How little we know of the Home Life of Shelley ; how greatly a Mrs. Joseph Severin might have supplemented our knowledge of Keats ! Years after Keats's death Browning passionately asked " What porridge had John Keats ? " He got no answer ; his legitimate curiosity was unsatisfied. Keats almost certainly ate porridge ; there must have been people who knew what kind of porridge. But they cared nothing for the needs of posterity ; they selfishly kept their knowledge to themselves. All we can do is to be thankful that we have now a full-length portrait of at least one of the great poets : pending anything further, we shall have to take him as a type of them all.

# CHRISTOPHER SMART

CHRISTOPHER SMART, author of the *Song to David*, was born at Shipbourne, Kent, on April 4, 1722. His family was North Country ; his father was steward in Kent to William, Lord Vane, younger son of Lord Barnard of Raby Castle, Durham. The poet was sent to school at Durham. His holidays were frequently spent at Raby Castle. His talents were noticed, and the connection resulted in his getting an allowance first from the Duchess of Cleveland, and then from Henry Vane, Earl of Darlington. In 1739 he was sent to Pembroke College, Cambridge, where he was contemporary with Gray. Gray was sober and fastidious, Smart something of a rioter and drunkard ; they did not become intimate, though Gray, when Smart was in distress, took pains to do him kindnesses. The turbulent undergraduate became in 1745 a dissipated Fellow. Perhaps it was merely that he chafed against surroundings where (in his words)

> discipline and dulness dwell
> And genius ne'er was seen to roam.

No sooner was he a Fellow than he scandalised the precise by making the undergraduates perform a comedy of his own composition, " A Trip to Cambridge," in the College Hall. In 1747 Gray writes :

His debts daily increase. . . . In the meantime he is amusing himself with a comedy of his

own writing, which he makes all the boys of his
acquaintance act. . . . Our friend, Lawman, the
mad attorney, is his copyist, and truly the author
himself is as mad as he. His piece, he says, is in-
imitable—true sterling wit and humour, by God,
and he can't hear the prologue without being
ready to die with laughter. He acts five parts himself, and is sorry he can't do all the rest. He has
also advertised a collection of odes, and for his
vanity and faculty of lying, they are come to their
full maturity. All this, you see, must come to a
jail or Bedlam, and that without help, almost
without pity.

The jail was narrowly escaped almost at once ;
Smart was arrested for a tailor's debt, and his
colleagues (who, like Gray, could not, it seems,
help taking an interest in him) saved him by a sub-
scription. In 1750 he won the Seatonian Prize for a
poem (the Prize still exists and is substantial) on the
Attributes of the Supreme Being. In 1751 Gray's
prediction came literally true. Gray is supposed to
be referring to Smart in a letter to Walpole, who
wanted an amanuensis : " We have a Man here
that writes a good Hand ; but he has two little Fail-
ings, that hinder my recommending him to you. He
is lousy, and he is mad : he sets out this week for
Bedlam ; but if you insist upon it, I don't doubt he
will pay his Respects to you." At all events to Bedlam
Smart went, with religious mania. He was let out
and at once—showing therein a prudence rare in
the lives of most authors and unique in his own
—married the daughter of a publisher. This,

ordinarily, would have been enough to lose him his Fellowship ; but Pembroke, lenient to him once more, told him he could keep it if he would go on writing Seatonian Poems. This he did, winning the prize in 1751, 1752, 1753, and 1755 ; but by that time he had gone to London and begun to write for the booksellers. He used the striking pseudonym of " Mary Midnight," and he edited a periodical (of which I should like to see a set) called " The Midwife, or the Old Woman's Magazine." For ten years he led a miserable life, deep in drink and debt. His family left him, and, developing mania again, he was sent back to the madhouse, where he spent two years. Johnson, who had always liked him, went to see him there. He thought that Smart was perhaps best off there, as he dug in the garden, whereas, before his confinement, all the exercise he got was a walk to the alehouse, " but he was carried back again." Nevertheless, Johnson did not think him mad enough to be in an asylum. " His infirmities were not noxious to society. He insisted upon people praying with him, and I'd as lief pray with Kit Smart as with anyone else." During that confinement he wrote the poem by which his name lives, a sudden burst into grandeur, the " Song to David," noblest perhaps of all English religious poems. They say he wrote it with a key on his door panels, pens and ink being denied him ; the story is without proof. There it is. Smart came out ; resumed his former occupations ; met the Burneys and borrowed money from them ; struck Fanny as having " great wildness in his manners, looks, and voice," and in 1770 died in the King's Bench Prison.

# CHRISTOPHER SMART

Smart's poems, except for one, have not I think been edited for over a century. There is no doubt at all that " The Song to David " was immeasurably the best of them, and that it had a quality found in nothing else of its age. So out of its surroundings was it that even those of Smart's contemporaries who admired his other work thought nothing of it. Dr. Johnson is not a case in point. He wrote a ludicrous parody of the " Song to David," catching the form and missing—but perhaps he wanted to miss—its blazing content ; but he thought nothing of Smart even when Smart was sane. It was when asked his view of the respective merits of Smart and Derrick that he made his celebrated remark (which might so often be justly applied to other controversies concerning authors), " Sir, there is no settling the point of precedency between a louse and a flea." But in 1791 Smart was edited in two volumes by an admirer, and from that edition the " Song to David " was omitted as the unfortunate lapse of a lunatic. It afforded, remarked the editor, " melancholy proofs of the recent estrangement of his mind." Just afterwards Anderson, compiling his " British Poets," came across six stanzas. He could not find a whole copy of the poem, and printed these six, remarking that " the slight defects and singularities of this neglected performance are amply compensated by a grandeur, a majesty of thought, and a happiness of expression." Chalmers reprinted the six stanzas and spoke of their " majestic animation"; and in 1819 the whole poem was reprinted by an anonymous admirer. Fifty years passed before it really came into its own ; but then its great qualities were fully realised. Rossetti wrote of it as " the only great accomplished poem of the last century. The unaccomplished ones are Chatterton's—of course, I mean earlier than Blake or Coleridge, and without reckoning so exceptional a genius as Burns. A master-piece of rich imagery, exhaustive resources, and reverberant sound." Browning made Smart one of the recipients of his " Parleyings with Certain People of Importance in their Day." He described him-self, exploring Smart's works (and, by implication, the eighteenth century), as one who goes through room after room in a great house where there is no lack of the signs of decent taste and adequate cul-ture, where

> All showed the Golden Mean without a hint
> Of brave extravagance that breaks the rule,

and who suddenly lifts a hanging and steps into a magnificently beautiful chapel, full of a profusion of audacious beauties. So with Smart :

> The man was sound
> And sane at starting : all at once the ground
> Gave way beneath his step, a certain smoke
> Curled up and caught him, or perhaps down broke
> A fireball wrapping flesh and spirit both
> In conflagration.

Critics usually exaggerate ; it is a pity to under-rate Gray's " Elegy " because it is not in the same kind as the " Song to David " and the writings of Blake ; even common sense and common tenderness have achieved their milder glories. Still Smart's poem does sweep one away as nothing else does that was written in its age, an age which employed the word " enthusiast " as a synonym for " maniac." Smart, in his cell, burning with a fierce fire of inspiration, rhapsodised like " the lunatic, the lover, and the poet " all in one. He saw the whole universe blazing with light and pulsing with adoration, and the very incoherence and inconsequence of his vivid apostrophes witness the intensity of his visionary frenzy. From a quiet beginning, contemplating the qualities of the ideal man, he rises, with quicker pulse, to a survey of the riches of God's earth, birds, beasts, and fishes, trees, flowers, and gems, until he breaks into the superbest hymn of praise in our language :

> For Adoration, in the skies,
> The Lord's philosopher espies
>     The Dog, the Ram, and Rose ;
> The planet's ring, Orion's sword ;
> Nor is his greatness less ador'd
>     In the vile worm that glows.

So he goes through a splendid catalogue. Then, with the repetitiveness of religious excitement, he utters stanza after stanza springing from certain epithets :

> Sweet is the dew that falls betimes
> And drops upon the leafy limes ;
>     Sweet Hermon's fragrant air :
> Sweet is the lily's silver bell,
> And sweet the wakeful tapers smell
>     That watch for early prayer. . . .

Sweeter in all the strains of love,
The language of thy turtle-dove,
    Pair'd to thy swelling chord ;
Sweeter with ev'ry grace endued,
The glory of thy gratitude,
    Respir'd unto the Lord.

Strong is the horse upon his speed ;
Strong in pursuit the rapid glede,
    Which makes at once his game ;
Strong the tall ostrich on the ground ;
Strong through the turbulent profound
    Shoots Xiphias to his aim.

Strong is the lion—like a coal
His eyeball—like a bastion's mole
    His chest against the foes :
Strong the gier eagle on his sail,
Strong against tide th' enormous whale
    Emerges, as he goes.

But stronger still in earth and air,
And in the sea, the man of prayer,
    And far beneath the tide,
And in the seat to faith assigned,
Where ask is have, where seek is find,
    Where knock is open wide. . . .

Shouting in exultation, he proceeds through stanza after stanza on this model until, with the " glorious" stanzas he reaches the most splendid peroration in English, concluding with the culminating act of salvation now at last

# CHRISTOPHER SMART

Determin'd, Dar'd, and Done.

What emphasis in the very sound of it ! Smart never did compose anything like that before or after; had this been his usual level he would have been one of the greatest of the world's poets. Yet critics have been rather unjust to his other work. Mr. Birrell is typical when he describes Smart as being " until he lost his reason a very indifferent versifier." Mr. Streatfield goes farther and remarks that " his poems —all save one—were the spiritless effusions of a literary hack." Some of them were ; but not all, unless the opinion be held that there can be no degrees of merit in anything so uniformly contemptible as eighteenth-century verse. Let it be admitted that most of Smart's poetry was written under constraint of an atmosphere which did not favour the more ardent kind of poetry, and that he might have done much more had he been born in another century. But even his more conventional verses are not devoid of poetic feeling or craftsmanship. His poem " On an Eagle Confined in a College Court " is worth a place in any anthology, energetic, eloquent, and precise. In the Odes, which Gray anticipated with so much disquiet, there are stilted things and passages which have been spoiled for us by the change in idiom—for instance, the salute to a bride as " egregious nymph ! " Modern taste, too, might reject such works as the " Ode on the Sudden Death of a Clergyman." But nothing could be more delicate, in the manner of the time, than the " Ode to Idleness," which begins :

Goddess of ease, leave Lethe's brink,
    Obsequious to the Muse and me ;
For once endure the pain to think,
    Oh ! sweet insensibility !

Sister of peace and indolence,
    Bring, Muse ! bring numbers soft and slow,
Elaborately void of sense,
    And sweetly thoughtless let them flow. . . .

The last two verses run :

For thee, O Idleness, the woes
    Of life we patiently endure,
Thou art the source whence labour flows,
    We shun thee but to make thee sure.

For who'd sustain war's toil and waste,
    Or who th' hoarse thund'ring of the sea,
But to be idle at the last,
    And find a pleasing end in thee ?

There is not only truth but humour in these pointed
lines. Humour may be found elsewhere—in Smart's
satirical work, in some of his charming ballads, in
the " Apology to a Lady for his being a Little Man."
It is sometimes found misplaced. He had the effron-
tery to write an Epilogue to " Othello," to be spoken
by Desdemona, which opens with :

True woman to the last—my peroration
I come to speak in spight of suffocation ;
To show the present and the age to come,
We may be choak'd, but never can be dumb.

# CHRISTOPHER SMART

His " Georgic," " The Hop-Garden," a eulogy of the best product of his native Kent, is an amusing burlesque in the Miltonic style. His invocation will give a notion of how close he gets to his model. He implores the help of John Philips, who had previously copied Milton :

> If thou, O Philips, fav'ring dost not hear
> Me, inexpert of verse ; with gentle hand
> Uprear the unpinion'd muse, high on the top
> Of that immeasurable mount, that far
> Exceeds thine own Plynlimmon, where thou tun'st
> With Phœbus' self thy lyre. Give me to turn
> Th' unwieldy subject with thy graceful ease,
> Extol its baseness with thy art ; but chief
> Illumine, and invigorate with thy fire.

Elsewhere in the poem a close and sympathetic observation of nature is shown ; as it is also in " A Morning Piece," " A Noon Piece," and " A Night Piece." These three poems do not resemble the " Song to David," but they are very charming. Smart mad was a great poet ; even sane he must have been a remarkably good companion in those taverns.